MAKING
the GRADE

How to Study at the College Level

REVISED EDITION

Mark Pruitt

Mark Pruitt
pruittmark@yahoo.com

ISBN: 1-4752-1888-5

ISBN-13: 978-1-4752-1888-6

Printed in the United States of America

Cover & layout design by Enrique Colón
enriquecolon@outlook.com

Because of the dynamic nature of the internet, any Web addresses or links contained
in this book may have changed since publication and may no longer be valid.

What others are saying ...

"Mark Pruitt's book is great, and I would recommend it to all my students. It would help all students live up to their potential as they move through their college career. Mark, congratulations on a well written and thoughtful book. I hope it is adopted and helps a whole generation of students."

Bob G. Figgins, PhD
Professor of Economics
College of Business & Global Affairs
University of Tennessee at Martin

"Finally, something that is helpful in a non-complicated language that the incoming freshman will understand."

Charles Savage
Assistant Professor of Music
Ohio University – Zanesville

"Mark Pruitt is knowledgeable, experienced, and has sound advice. This book will be helpful to student readers."

Cathy Quenin, PhD, CCC-SLP
Professor & Chair
Communication Sciences & Disorders
Nazareth College

"Congratulations on an excellent book. I believe it could be very helpful to today's college students."

Ron Highfield
Blanche E. Seaver Professor of Religion
Pepperdine University

"*Making the Grade* is an appropriate required purchase for all in-coming freshmen. It is both interesting *and* helpful, and its short, easy-to-read lessons are applicable to the busy college student and professional."

Tanya Enloe, M.S., CCC-SLP
Assistant Professor
Communication Sciences & Disorders
Valdosta State University

About the author |

Mark enjoys being part of the college scene and making a difference in the lives of students. He has been on a college campus for over fifteen years and has spent the majority of that time serving as Assistant Director of Admissions for Harding University in Searcy, AR. He and his wife Kim have three extraordinary children – Maggie, Phoenix, and Luke.

Making the Grade
Contents

I. Early Orientation

II. Pruitt's Course on Study Skills

III. Pruitt's Course on Time Management

IV. Pruitt's Course on College Life

Thank you

Several people have helped make this book a reality, but I would specifically like to thank the following people for the special contributions they have made. Without their help, this book would have never gotten off the ground.

I want to send out a special "Thank You!" to my International Relations professor who gave me the inspiration for this book. Thank you, Professor, for putting on my transcript what I had earned. Had I received an "A" in your class, I most likely would never have been upset enough to develop these study techniques, and therefore, never would have written this book.

Thank you, Kim, for being a wonderful wife and being so gracious and supportive during the many hours I have spent on this project. I know you are the real author in this family, but it has been a fun experience writing this and having you by my side.

Thank you, Maggie, Phoenix, and Luke, for being wonderful children! You make life as a daddy extremely enjoyable, and God couldn't have blessed us with better children.

Thank you to my parents, Lynn and Emma Mae Pruitt, and my in-laws, Dale and Bobbie Ross, who have always stood by us and have given us tons of support. Thank you so much!

Thank you, Dr. Cole Bennett. You have been a long-time friend and have been so good to help by editing this book.

Dr. Michael Claxton, thank you for stepping in for additional editing when I needed you. I am very grateful.

Thank you, Ricky Colón, for doing all the graphic design work. You are very talented, and I appreciate your help.

❖ ❖ ❖

Harvey Mackay, I love your books and your writing style. You have helped inspire me to write a book of my own. Thank you.

❖ ❖ ❖

Jeffrey J. Fox, your books have also been a great example for me. Thank you.

❖ ❖ ❖

I'd also like to thank all of you students and parents who have kept asking me how my book was coming along and when it would be available. You have kept me on task, and your interest in *Making the Grade* has been very encouraging.

❖ ❖ ❖

And thank you, reader, for picking up a copy of this book. Your faith in me as a mentor means a lot, and I deeply value your business as well. If you find that this book helps you in your quest for deeper learning and for obtaining great grades in the classroom, please forward it on to some of your friends. Maybe I can help them, too.

EARLY ORIENTATION

 # Early Orientation |

Preface
(But You Should Read This Anyway)

Welcome to *Making the Grade*. I know your time is short, and you're wondering if this book is even worth reading. My guess is you are either struggling with your grades, or you're wanting to know how to save your scholarship and keep your parents off your back, or you are simply trying to maximize your time to get the most out of your learning experience. You want to do well in school, but you don't want to take a class on how to study, and you certainly don't want a book on studying that requires a PhD just to read! Well, read on, my friend. I think I can help you.

I am Assistant Director of Admissions for a private university in the South, and I have been on a college campus for over fifteen years. My goal is simple: To quickly and effectively help you get the most out of your college learning and help you have the ultimate college experience. I want to help you learn how to study effectively and do so in the least amount of *your* time. This book is not long, it is easy to read, and it can make a difference in your study results immediately. In fact, if you want to know the secret to getting the most out of your studying and earning great grades in college, then go straight to Lesson 9 and learn **The 4 Study Steps**. That's it! If you will diligently follow **The 4 Study Steps**, you'll be well on your way to dominating your classes. I do, however, encourage you to read the other lessons before and after

Lesson 9 because they contain key information and cool techniques to help you get the most out of **The 4 Study Steps** and to help you learn what you were meant to learn.

Technology also plays a big part in education today and will continue to evolve in the coming years. You will notice that my illustrations assume an on-campus experience with a live professor. With many online classes today, you may at first consider my techniques outdated. However, no matter the medium, there will always be lessons to read, information to study, and projects to work on. So, although **The 4 Study Steps** and the techniques discussed in this book worked for me with a live professor, they still apply today for online classes, podcasts, webinars, and other new educational media.

Lesson 1 |

Early Orientation
An Introduction

E arning great grades in college is a worthy goal, and I commend you for that desire. But, as you are probably aware, getting an "A" in a class does not necessarily mean you have learned the material. There were several times throughout my academic career when I crammed the night before a test and got an "A," but I know I did not truly learn what I was supposed to learn. I want to stress here, at the beginning, that learning is much more important than getting an "A" in a class. For example, according to one of my professor friends, if a "D" student works hard and raises his or her grade level to a "C," there is great reason to celebrate because the student has demonstrated a higher competency and ability on the subject.[1] This student may not have earned an "A" in the class, but success was achieved.

You need to understand that there are no shortcuts to learning and there are no quick and easy gimmicks to increase your knowledge in any subject matter. I am not going to promise or guarantee that if you follow my recommendations, you will automatically graduate at the top of your class. However, I believe that any student, no matter what his or her background, no matter what the level of academic success in the past, can achieve a higher level of learning, and therefore, should be able to earn grades in the classroom that accurately reflect that level of learning. Throughout this book I talk about earning an "A" in a class, and my illustrations also exemplify earning an "A" versus a lower grade. Please note that learning is the main objective, and these illustrations are simply illustrations and should not be taken as a guarantee. Also note that I am not suggesting that any grade less than an "A" equals failure. However, I must admit that when I finally learned how to study correctly, a whole new world opened up to me. I was able to truly master the classroom material, earn a 95% or higher in every class, and still have fun with my friends. I want you to be able to have the same amazing college experience I had. This book is the culmination of the techniques I learned and developed when I finally figured out how to study correctly, and I hope it can make a positive contribution to your college experience as well.

The inspiration for this book came over Christmas break of my junior year of college, when I had just received a grade in my International Relations class that was extremely aggravating. The class consisted of 1,000 total available points, and the grading scale was as follows:

$$A = 900 - 1000, B = 800 - 899, C = 700 - 799,$$

$$D = 600 - 699, F = 0 - 599$$

The professor also gave students the benefit of the doubt if they were within ten points of the cutoff. For example, a student who earned 790 points would receive a "B-," or if a student earned 890, he gave him or her an "A-." When the dust settled at the end of my final exam, I had a total score of 8...8...9. I missed an "A-" by one point! Not one percentage point, but one single, solitary point! I was hacked. Sure, a "B+" wasn't bad, but one more point could have gotten me an "A-." And coming that close, yet missing the mark, was so frustrating!

I was initially upset with my professor, but it really wasn't his fault. After all, I am the one who took the quizzes and tests and earned the points. He was gracious enough to bump up those students who were on the fence, so I really couldn't blame him. But I was so angry at the time that I had to do something. I wanted revenge, and I needed to send a clear message to the university that it wouldn't soon forget. So, over Christmas break, I came up with the perfect plan. My retaliation? *Learn the material so thoroughly and get straight "A's" the following semester.* Oh, yeah. That would show 'em! They'd think twice before putting another "B" on my transcript.

But, to pull off this "Mother of All Retaliations," my study habits had to undergo a major overhaul. The way I took notes, the way I studied those notes, and the way I used my time all had to change. Waiting until the last minute to open the books was about to become a thing of the past.

Initially, I thought I needed to spend more time studying, but when I considered my upcoming semester and how busy it was going to be, I wasn't sure I could pull it off. I had a job of being in charge of a men's dorm, I was on the school's intercollegiate business team, I was an officer in two or three organizations, and I was the drummer for a jazz combo that traveled to several places to perform. I had also signed up to take seventeen credit hours that next semester. As you can see, my schedule was going to be extremely tight, so I couldn't just free up more time to study. But what I could do was make sure I used whatever time I had well. I began to develop a study method that I had never used before—a study method that would ensure I would really learn the material in the short time I had available. And, I must admit, it worked extremely well. It is composed of a single study strategy and several study techniques that are explained in detail throughout this book. I named the strategy **The 4 Study Steps**, and it became the foundation for my academic success.

By following **The 4 Study Steps**, I did make straight "A's" that spring semester and learned the material better than I ever had in the past. I even earned 107% in Business Law II (make sure you read

Lesson 19 on how to take advantage of extra credit opportunities) and I'm sure the academic deans are still talking about it. Yes, I was able to get the last laugh, but I soon realized that maybe I shouldn't keep the laughter to myself. Maybe some other students could use this information to get some laughter into their lives.

What started as a frustration for not getting an "A" had turned into a study method that vastly improved my college experience. I was able to be very active in campus events, have fun with my friends, and still make a 95% or higher in every class. My stress level went way down, and–I know this may sound hard to believe–it was actually fun taking tests. That's right. It was actually fun taking tests because I knew exactly what was going to be on each one. Did I cheat? Of course not. I finally learned how to study and it made all the difference. Again, I'm not going to guarantee that you will make "A's" in all of your classes or that your life will be stress-free and absolutely perfect. But, if you follow this method diligently, you should be able to improve your grades and increase your level of learning. You should also be able to spend plenty of time with your friends to help make your college experience the best years yet.

Lesson 2 |

The Ground Rules

N ow, before we get into the specifics on how to deepen your level of learning and achieve great grades at the college level, there are some key concepts you should be aware of and also some things you need to know concerning how this book is arranged. One of those key concepts is the difference between high school and college, and we will cover this in the next two lessons. Another key concept is how your brain works, which is the subject of Lessons 5 and 6. In Lesson 7, we talk about the Study Zone and the monumental role it plays in your studying success and how to find the best spot for you.

Lesson 9 is the main lesson where we learn **The 4 Study Steps**. I will refer to **The 4 Study Steps** quite often throughout these lessons, and it is imperative that you follow these steps completely and in the proper order. That's very important, so I'm going to say it again. It is imperative that you follow **The 4 Study Steps** completely and in the proper order. I also suggest committing them to memory, and, since there are only four, that should be fairly easy to do. You will notice that I have bolded **The 4 Study Steps** throughout the entire text and have included each Study Step icon, where appropriate, to help you recognize them and to help your mind assimilate them in the correct sequence. Once you get in the habit of doing them each day, they will become an integral part of your college life.

Beginning with Lesson 10, I have arranged the remaining lessons in the Course on Study Skills in an order consistent with **Study Steps 1–3**, going from the first day of class to the final exam. The majority of those lessons dealing with **Study Step 4** are found later in the book in the Course on Time Management.

A phrase you will see several times throughout the book is the Dreaded Project. The Dreaded Project is any big project or homework assignment that you really don't want to do. It may be a presentation, or a 10-page paper, or any assignment that you, well, dread. Every class seems to have a Dreaded Project of some sort, and although you would almost rather die than have to complete it, you're still going to have to complete it. However, I will give you several tips on how to conquer the Dreaded Project and turn in something you're proud of.

There are numerous study techniques presented in this book, and it is ideal if you start these techniques on the first day of the semester. However, that may be a little difficult for you if it's late in the school year and you are just now discovering this book. The important thing to remember is to start immediately, no matter where you are in the semester. If you are in your first week of classes or on the verge of finals, don't put off these study techniques another day. Like all good habits, it is better to have started months or years ago. But no matter what your situation, by all means, start NOW!

PRUITT'S COURSE
on STUDY SKILLS

Lesson 3 |

A Few Differences
Between High School and College

I had a great high school experience, but as I look back on both my high school years and my college years, I can easily say that my college years were much more fun and fulfilling than high school ever was. This is a critical stage in your life, and the biggest adjustment you will make during this time is the transition from being under your parents' direction to charting a direction of your own. Most of you have probably not lived an extended time outside of your parents' home and it is going to be an adjustment at first. It may be a little weird not having Mom or Dad waking you up and making sure you get to class on time, or cooking your meals, or telling you what to do. It's definitely a transition that is going to take some getting used to.

But, the main difference I want to focus on is the difference in the classroom. If in high school you could get by on your brains alone, be prepared for a change. That will probably not happen in college. Having brains is not going to hurt you, by any means, but making great grades without studying is not likely to be a reality. You should be another year closer to adulthood as you head off to college and this maturity will be expected of you. The classroom material is usually a lot more in-depth–and the expectations by the professor a lot more demanding–than what you were used to in high school. There is also a ton of reading in nearly every college class, and you won't want to fall behind.

It is true that some of your college classes may seem easy to you because you may have had a great teacher in high school who covered the same material. I remember taking General Physics in college with a friend of mine from high school. This was a neat scenario because a few years earlier, Steve and I sat in the same Physics class in high school, and since we had an excellent teacher the first time around, it was enjoyable taking the same class at the college level. We both made high grades and it was a very interesting class.

Most classes at the college level, however, are going to be quite a bit tougher than high school. But that's the way it should be. After all, it is college. The professor will cover a lot of material in a lot less time than what you were used to, and he or she may not even want to stop for questions. Calculus I was the first class of my college career and it met at 8:00 every morning. I can still remember the words of the professor on the very first day: "This first unit is going to be review for most of you, so let's just breeze right through it." Well, I didn't have the luxury of taking Calculus in high school, so I definitely was not counted in the "most of you" category. I barely pulled a "C" out of that class and it was quite miserable. However, I did meet one of my best friends, Troy, in that class and from him I met four of my closest friends. So, I guess that class wasn't all a bad experience, but it was really discouraging to have the professor go a lot faster than what I was prepared for. Two years passed before I finally learned how to study correctly, and that knowledge sure would have been helpful that first semester when I was making the transition from high school to college.

Another thing I was a little naïve about when I went to college was the attitude of some of the students. I thought that since I was now in college, where the grades really mattered and the academic competition and price were considerably higher than that of my high school, every student would hit the books every night and do his or her very best. Man, was I in for a surprise! I found that a lot of students did not come to college to study, but merely to have a good time. Many spent more time going out, playing computer games, or watching television than they did in their books, and their grades showed it. So, when you go off to school, be aware that there will be students from all different backgrounds and many will have different goals than you.

College is a great place to have fun *and* to learn. But, if you think getting a good education and doing well in school means sacrificing the "best years of your life," then think again. I hope the techniques discussed in this book can help you do both.

Lesson 4 |

Leave the Past Behind

Good news! Whatever your performance level was in high school, it doesn't really matter. If you didn't do so hot with the grades, or if you have to lower your voice when someone asks you what you made on the ACT or SAT, don't sweat it. Most employers and graduate schools are not going to put much weight on how well you did in high school, so when you get to college, you can start all over. If you achieved less than your potential earlier, you now have another chance to do it right.

By the same token, if you were the top dog in high school, don't assume that success will automatically come your way at the next level. There are some fairly sharp students who assemble at colleges all across the country, many of whom were the top dogs at their high school. As a result, the level of academic competition will be quite a bit higher than it was at the prep level just a year before.

So, leave the Ghost of High School Past behind you and gear up for a fresh, new start.

Lesson 5 |

A Gallon of Milk

Ever since elementary school, I've been a conscientious and competitive student. This academic competition carried on into junior high and then into high school, where I dove into extra-curricular activities such as basketball, band, chorus, swing choir, jazz band, and forensics. It was at this point that I noticed the time available for studying seemed to virtually disappear. Basketball practice would sometimes run late, an upcoming music competition would need additional preparation, and then there would be a Physics test in two days that I hadn't even started studying for! All these activities seemed to crash into each other. To survive, I simply stayed up really late the night before every test and just crammed it all in. Sound familiar?

This "Night Before" method of studying stayed with me as I headed off to college because it was all I knew. However, there were a few problems with the "Night Before" method. First of all, it was consistently very stressful. I would have an upcoming test that I was not in the least bit prepared for or I had a project that I should have been working on, and those nagging thoughts were always in the back of my mind. I couldn't get rid of them. But, because I lacked the proper discipline, I didn't do anything about them until it was nearly too late. And, by then, the stress had built up and become so overwhelming that I couldn't concentrate on anything else.

Another problem with cramming the night before a test was that the information didn't stick around long enough to make itself at home. If you were to test me over the same material a week later, I would have to re-invite all the information back to my brain and cram it all in again. Why? Because I never really learned the material the first time. Your brain is an amazing organ, but I don't think it was made to receive a whole bunch of new material in a short period of time and hold it in forever, or at least where you can recall the information readily.

The best analogy I can think of to describe the "Night Before" method is to use a gallon of milk. I once witnessed several guys who challenged themselves to drink a gallon of whole or 2% milk in one hour. If (and I mean *if*) they drank it all in one hour, they had to hold it in until the hour was complete. Only one person of the group successfully completed this feat, but a mere four seconds after the hour was up—Niagara Falls, baby! Out it came. Your brain works in the same fashion...sort of. When you cram everything in the night before a test, you can only hold the information in for so long before it's gone.

If this "Night Before" study method and time management system sound all too familiar to you, you are in for a change that will drastically cut back on your stress level and will increase your level of learning and recall ability. No more cramming the night before a test. Yay! If you diligently follow **The 4 Study Steps**, you should be able to go to bed at a decent hour, if you want to, and feel really good about it.

Lesson 6 |

The Window of Recovery

B ased on my own experience, I have found that there is a small window of time (I'd say about three hours) where the material from class can really sink into your brain. I call this the Window of Recovery, and the key is to review the material thoroughly at least once before that window closes.[2] Please note that the earlier you get to studying the notes, the stronger the material will be reinforced. For example, studying your notes within twenty minutes of class will be more effective than two hours after class. Both study times are within the Window of Recovery, but getting to those notes sooner will definitely pay off. Waiting until next week, or even the next day, to study your notes definitely will not.

Now, most of you will probably have several classes in a row, or you may have to go to work or to practice of some sort when your classes are over. If this is the case, getting to your notes before the Window of Recovery closes may seem somewhat close to impossible. However, there is a way to do it, and I show you how in Lessons 13, 26, and 34.

Lesson 6
Summary:

- Window of Recovery = the first three hours after class.

- Study your notes thoroughly before the three hours are up.

- Studying your notes sooner is always better than later.

Lesson 7 |

Your Study Zone

In order for you to excel in the classroom, one of the first things you will need to do is find a Study Zone. What is a Study Zone? A Study Zone is simply the place where you go to study. It needs to be a location that is free from distraction, easy to get to, and the place you go to study every day.

The library is usually a good place for a Study Zone, but when I was in college, our school library had a large room with rows and rows of tables for students to sit at and study. We did everything *but* study. I'd get to talking to my friends, or this guy at the next table would be doing something really funny and the whole group of us would start laughing. I could easily spend over an hour in that library and have nothing to show for it. I ended up going back to my dorm room and found that I could get tons more accomplished there. That school library has since been renovated and is a lot more conducive to studying, but when I was there, it was not a good location for my Study Zone.

◆ **Your Study Zone needs to be free from distraction.**

Go where there is no TV, no music blaring, and no friends to talk to. I'd even consider putting your phone on "silent." Good studying needs to take place at this location and you need your mind to be free from wandering thoughts and distractions.

Let me warn you about taking a blanket outside and spending a beautiful afternoon on the front lawn to study. There are way too many distractions at your disposal. Even if there are no people or animals around, nature is full of constant movement and noises. A slight breeze will come up, moving the trees and bushes...and also your papers. Birds will sing, a bug will crawl on your blanket, or a fly will buzz around your head. There will be too much sunlight or not enough sunlight. The temperature will change, making it too warm or too cold to focus.

Add humans into the mix and your distractions are guaranteed. Even if no one comes over to talk to you, it is nearly impossible to fully concentrate while studying outside. People make noise. Some will have dogs that run and bark. People will talk, they will laugh, and they will yell to their friends. And then, there will be some who might even want to come over and talk to you. I'm telling you, it's very difficult to get much studying done outside. Granted, it's nearly impossible to get away from all noises and distractions completely, but my experience has shown that studying inside in a quiet room is far more productive than going outside.

Also, study with other people only as a last resort. If you can't grasp the concepts, go see your professor first. If that route isn't available, track down a trustworthy classmate. Otherwise, go it alone. You'll get more accomplished and your time will be effectively spent. And, if you are physically attracted to someone, I'd advise not studying with that particular person either. If you are trying to impress him or her, that's one thing. But if you are trying to actually get some studying done, don't do it. You'll find yourself concentrating more on how you can make a suave move and less on your books. Trust me. It's much more productive to study by yourself.

This may be more than you bargained for, but I want to add one additional note about TV and music. Some people claim they have to have the TV on or their favorite music playing in order to concentrate.

Studies have shown that having this sort of media on in the background can actually be dangerous to your mind.[3] Your subconscious mind is extremely powerful; so powerful, in fact, that we actually become what is embedded in our subconscious mind.

When your conscious mind is focused on a particular television program or certain song, if there is questionable content, your mind can refute it. But when your conscious mind is not concentrating on the television show or music playing in the background (like when you are focused on studying), your conscious mind does not refute it. Instead, your subconscious mind absorbs it and stores that picture forever. Your subconscious mind is constantly working and assimilating all the pictures that is stored in its memory, and that is who you are at this particular moment.

You've heard it said that you become what you think about. That is exactly right. If you want to change your circumstances, then change what goes into your mind, especially your subconscious mind. Want to perform better? Want to get better grades? Put pure, powerful, and positive messages into your subconscious mind and watch your life transform.[4] You may think I'm blowing smoke, but go ask your Psychology professor and find out for yourself.

If you need to have "white noise" to tune out some of the other distractions, try listening to classical music. For me, classical music is great because there are usually no lyrics and I'm not tempted to sing along. I've even heard some people swear that listening to Mozart's music will actually make you smarter. I can't promise that one, but I can tell you that my copy of *Mozart's Greatest Hits* sure got a lot of playing time when I was in school. If classical music doesn't appeal to you, try turning on your fan instead of your TV.

Basically, all I'm saying is that it is rather difficult to fully concentrate when you have a bunch of background noise going on. If you must listen to something while you study, make sure it has positive, uplifting content.

◆ **Your Study Zone needs to be easy to get to.**

It would be ideal if you could get away from all the noise and distractions on a college campus to get your studying done. However, if you have to travel over ten minutes to get to your ideal place of study, I would reconsider that location and try to find a new place. You are going to spend a lot of time at your Study Zone, so find a place that is relatively easy to get to on a daily basis.

◆ **You need to go to your Study Zone every day.**

Yes, every day. Good studying is a way of life for the college student, and the best way to learn the material is to go over it daily, even on weekends. When you first find your Study Zone, you may discover that, although it is a quiet place, you may not get much accomplished. That's okay. Keep at it. It won't take long for your brain to be "at home" in this location, and you will soon find that you will be able to get into study mode faster and will be able to focus for longer periods of time.

....

Lesson 7
Summary:

....

◆ Your Study Zone is the place where you do
most of your studying.

◆ Your Study Zone needs to be free from distraction.

◆ Your Study Zone needs to be easy to get to.

◆ Go to your Study Zone every day.

Lesson 8 |

The Stuff That Counts

I f you want to deepen your level of learning and make great grades in college, there are really only two main ingredients you need: Discipline and Desire. That's about what it boils down to. It's not how well you did in high school, or how high you scored on the ACT or SAT, or even your IQ level. If you have enough discipline and if you want it bad enough, not only can you make it through college, but you may make it through with honors and really surprise some people.

So, don't worry if your grades have been less than impressive up to this point, or if your test scores didn't qualify you for a scholarship, or if your friends and family members have their doubts. You can do this! Just put some of that Discipline and Desire to work and let's get started.

Lesson 9 |

The Stuff It Takes to Make the All-Stars:
The 4 Study Steps

O kay, here it is! This is the lesson you have been waiting for—the information to make all your dreams come true. So, without further delay, I present to you **The 4 Study Steps**. As I have previously mentioned, it is imperative that you follow these steps completely and in the proper order. Also note that each of these Study Steps will be covered in greater detail throughout the book.

STUDY STEP 1:

Go to class, pay attention, and take great notes.

Your class notes are the foundation to your success, so it is critical that you put forth solid effort in this area. You are in college to learn how to do something useful and marketable in this world, and college professors can teach you most of what you need to know to get you started. In order for you to learn, however, you have to listen and apply what they are telling you. Most people I know do not have supernatural recall ability by which they can remember every bit of information presented to them. Most people I know have to start writing down a grocery list on paper if it's going to be more than three items. Why? Because they can't readily recall everything they want to, when they want to. Remember the gallon of milk story? Your brain has a perfect photographic memory, but recalling the information when you want it is the tricky part. Writing things down will greatly enhance your recall ability, as opposed to merely listening.[5]

Let's look at the three simple directions to **Study Step 1** more closely.

GO TO CLASS

Don't ever think you can learn the material through osmosis, your friends' notes, or your exceptional brain power. You can't learn the material when you are absent...period. Do yourself a favor. Go to class.

PAY ATTENTION

Do not go to class to talk to your friends. If you want to talk, your friends will be available later. I guarantee it. I also recommend sitting near the front of the classroom. This allows you to hear the professor clearly and to read things the professor puts on the board or screen. Sitting near the front also helps eliminate distractions.

Also, do not use your phone during class. It is impossible to text and pay attention at the same time. Keep your phone off or on "silent" so you won't be tempted to text or be distracted by incoming messages and so you won't be rude while the professor is talking.

If you have trouble staying awake in class, you're going to need to find a way to change that. Get some caffeine or splash cold water on your face before class because if you are dozing off, you are going to miss some valuable information.

TAKE GREAT NOTES

Great note-taking entails paying attention and writing down pertinent information in ways that you will be able to follow, especially after class is over. I have included two entire lessons on note-taking to help you (see Lessons 10 and 11). Some professors will go fairly quickly and will present information faster than you can write down the concepts or type them into your computer. If you find yourself having a hard time keeping up, meet with the professor after class and get your questions answered that day. You may also want to bring a dictation recorder to class and listen to the lecture again later. But, as I said before, taking great notes is going to be the backbone to your success in the classroom, so don't take it lightly.

 # STUDY STEP 2:

Go straight to your Study Zone and study your notes immediately, thoroughly, and in order; study all previous days' notes.

 GO STRAIGHT TO YOUR STUDY ZONE

I am highly in favor of having a good time with your friends and making long-lasting memories, but there is a time and a place for all of that and right after class is definitely NOT the time. Go straight to your Study Zone when class is over and get started on **Study Step 2**.

STUDY YOUR NOTES IMMEDIATELY

You just spent good energy taking great notes in class; don't let it go to waste. Start studying immediately. The information will never be fresher than right after class, so the longer you wait to review your notes, the harder it will be to master them. In fact, if you get to your notes soon after class, mastering your notes should be relatively quick and easy because the material is so fresh in your mind.

Ideally, you should start studying your notes as soon as the professor says, "Class dismissed." You should go straight to your Study Zone and conquer the material. However, if this is not feasible, then you need to get to your Study Zone as soon as your schedule allows.

If you can't get to your Study Zone immediately after class, you had better have a good reason. Being tired and needing a break are not good reasons. Immediately after class is *the* key time of day to really make a difference in your grades. So, don't go to the Student Center, watch TV, or take a nap. If you do, you will seriously jeopardize your success. Study your notes immediately, and you will make your success so much easier.

In fact, you will probably soon realize that nothing exciting happens right after class anyway. You may get out of class around 2:00 – 4:00 pm, and if there is anything going on that night, like a concert, sporting event, or social function, it usually won't start until 7:00 pm or later. So, assuming you eat dinner (dinner *is* a great time to interact with your friends), this still gives you two to four hours of great study time. By getting started immediately after class, you could have a lot of your studying done *before* evening so you can really enjoy yourself later on.

STUDY YOUR NOTES THOROUGHLY

To study your notes thoroughly means to conquer or master whatever concept the professor was trying to get across. There are no shortcuts to learning, so make sure you know everything that was discussed in class. If you have lists to memorize, memorize them at this point. If you have concepts to learn, learn them now. If you have any question about what the professor was talking about, go take care of it by either emailing the professor or going to his or her office. Don't wait until tomorrow because you will have slept by then and you won't remember everything you need to remember.

STUDY YOUR NOTES IN ORDER

To study your notes in order simply means to study the notes from your first class of the day first, then the notes from your second class, then the notes from your third class, etc. Doing this helps you get to your first class as early as possible, ensuring that the Window of Recovery will not close on that set of notes. This is not rocket science, but it will help your recall ability and will help keep things organized.

STUDY ALL PREVIOUS DAYS' NOTES

This little step is your money maker! It is huge, and it means exactly what it says. To illustrate: On Day 2 of your class, after you have studied Day 2's notes thoroughly and in order, _go back and study Day 1's notes_. This is crucial because it will really reinforce what you studied the day before. And then on Day 3, after you have studied Day 3's notes thoroughly and in order, _go back and study Day 1's notes and Day 2's notes_. Are you getting the picture? Every day, you go over each previous day's set of notes. In other words, by the fifteenth day of the class, you are studying Day 15's set of notes, plus all the notes from the previous fourteen days. _Every day, you need to study every day's set of notes!_

Why go to all this trouble? Remember, there are no shortcuts to learning. Going over all previous days' set of notes on a daily basis magnifies your recall ability and does so in the least amount of time.[6] I know this process sounds like it will take forever, but you will be pleasantly surprised. It won't take much time at all. If you really followed through each day and took the effort to understand the concepts being presented and memorized whatever you needed to memorize, etc., it should all come back to you just by glancing over the earlier notes.

STUDY STEP 3:
....

Do your reading.

Classes in college are going to require a lot of reading, and if you get behind, it will be nearly impossible to catch up. So, do your reading the day it is assigned and don't get behind.

As you know, the professor has the right to put something on a test that may not have been covered in a lecture. If it's in the reading, it's fair game. But, if you keep up with your reading, you should be able to handle those particular questions, as well as any pop quizzes or bonus discussion questions that may come up.

By the way, a lot of what the professor talks about will most likely be found in detail in your textbook. By paying close attention in class and taking great notes **(Study Step 1)**, you will make those 40-200 pages that you have to read outside of class a lot easier to get through.

STUDY STEP 4:

*Complete any homework assignments
or work on projects.*

Keep up with any homework assignments you may have because they usually reinforce whatever concept was presented in class. And, when the end of the semester rolls around, those homework points can really come in handy.

Study Step 4 also involves working on any Dreaded Project that has been assigned for a minimum of 15 minutes every day. You probably will have at least one class each semester that has some sort of Dreaded Project that will be due later in the semester. Spend some time each day working on it, and that project won't be nearly the headache you thought it was. You'll be way ahead of the game.

By going through each of **The 4 Study Steps** completely and on a daily basis, you will greatly enhance your chance for success. On the night before a test, when you used to stay up until 4:00 am trying to cram everything in, you should now be able to watch the ball game or your favorite television shows and eat a pizza with your friends—stress-free. You should now be able to go to bed *before* midnight...totally prepared.

Lesson 9
Summary:

Study Step 1:
Go to class, pay attention, and take great notes.

Study Step 2:
Go straight to your Study Zone and study your notes immediately, thoroughly, and in order; study all previous days' notes.

Study Step 3:
Do your reading.

Study Step 4:
Complete any homework assignments or work on projects.

Lesson 10 |

Note-taking, The Art of – Part I

Study **Step 1** involves taking great notes in class, and, as I mentioned earlier, taking great notes is going to be the backbone of your success in the classroom. Why? Because, by taking great notes, you are forced to truly focus on, and listen intently to, what the professor is saying.

Now, before we get into the art of taking great notes, let me take a moment to address the "Typing notes on the laptop vs. Writing notes by hand" issue. We've come a long way in the last several years and laptops in some classrooms are commonplace. It wasn't too long ago when you were considered pretty hot stuff to have your own personal desktop that you didn't have to share with the rest of the family. Now, if you don't have your own laptop, you may feel a little out of place. Laptops are everywhere and they're great. I don't think I could function without mine.

However, it is my opinion that there is something special about writing things down on paper. It's as if something magical takes place when things are written by hand. Take, for example, the advice of goal-setting guru, Brian Tracy. Tracy is an internationally-known author and speaker, specializing in sales, leadership, business strategy, and managerial effectiveness. In his seminar, "The Psychology of Achievement," Tracy says that the best way to accomplish your goals is to actually write them down on paper. Once they are written, your mind instantly goes to work to accomplish them. That is amazing! And he emphasizes that writing the goal down on paper is much more effective than simply reading the goal.[7] Could the same phenomenon carry over to note-taking? Could the actual writing of classroom notes help lock those concepts into your brain in a way that typing the same notes cannot?

When I conducted my research on this issue, I found lots of articles supporting both sides. But, I must admit, there were more that preferred typing the class notes instead of writing them out. And, why not? The reasoning is valid: It's easier and faster to type than to write, making it easier to follow the discussion of the professor. I know all of that. I know it is easier to type, but when it comes to learning, easier is not necessarily better. So, if you just got your new laptop and you want to show it off by typing your notes in class, that's fine. I just recommend that you take the time after class to write those notes by hand into an actual old-school notebook.

With that said, how does one take great notes? You might want to check out additional note-taking sources such as "Penn State Learning,"[8] but here are some note-taking tips that I have found useful.

1A. <u>Write what is important to the professor.</u>

If the professor says, "You may want to write this down," that's usually a good indication that it needs to be found in your notebook. Also, whatever the professor puts on the board or screen should also be written down. For instance, let's say your literature professor, Dr. Wright, lists in a slide presentation the major differences between the writing styles of William Wordsworth and Walt Whitman. You'd better believe those items will show up in a multiple choice or essay question later on, so you'd better write them down.

2A. <u>Write as much as you can.</u>

It's better to write down too much information than not enough. Even if Dr. Wright supplies a note outline, don't just fill in the blanks and obvious points. Write extra notes to help you remember everything she discusses. What you don't want to happen is to come to a test question later on, knowing that you heard Dr. Wright talk about this topic once before, but not be able to remember what she said.

3A. <u>Write notes in your own words.</u>

This will ensure that you truly understand what the professor says. Learn to write with small phrases and abbreviations that you will recognize and remember later. However, if restating the professor's thoughts into your own words causes you to fall behind, then just write down the professor's words. Later, when you are going over your notes, change the professor's words into your own.

4A. <u>The "Already in the Textbook/Handout" Dilemma.</u>

Let's say Dr. Wright discusses the Wordsworth/Whitman differences and lists them in her slide presentation. You notice that the same list is included in your textbook on page 197 or on the hardcopy of notes Dr. Wright gives you. Do you need to write anything down in your notebook? For the moment, a simple note stating "See p. 197" or "See Handout" should suffice. However, I must issue a little warning here. When the information you need is already printed somewhere else (like in the textbook or on a handout), there is an easy tendency to let your mind relax. After all, why should you take the time to write things down that are already printed? This rationale could be a costly mistake. Continue to listen intently and write down as much as you can as she expands on each item. You may even want to take it one step further and rewrite the handout notes later into your notebook. Again,

I think an amazing thing happens when you take the time to write something down. I believe it helps lock the information into your head, making it much easier to recall later.

5A. <u>Come prepared.</u>

As you may recall, **Study Step 3** is to do your reading. Keeping up with your reading will not only help you learn the material, but it will also aid you in taking great notes. Much of what the professor talks about in class is probably found in the textbook, and completing your reading assignments before the lecture will allow you to follow the class discussions more easily. Remember, there is a strategy to learning and getting the best grades possible, and part of that strategy is to use your time wisely. Coming to class prepared will really pay off.

6A. <u>Don't be late.</u>

Have you ever gone to a movie only to find that you missed the first five minutes? How frustrating! You don't know who is who or what in the world is going on. If you could, you'd probably leave and come back for the late show. The same thing happens when you are late for class. Once the lecture starts, it can be very difficult to figure out what's going on. But, unlike the movies, that lecture does not have a late show. So, don't be late.

7A. <u>Get extra help if necessary.</u>

If you find yourself getting totally lost, or even remotely lost, during class, get with Dr. Wright as quickly as you can. Wait around after class if you need to or meet her in her office. Whatever it takes, don't go to sleep until you get the information and understand the material. If you have the professor's permission, another option is to record her lectures using a dictation recorder that you can buy at most office supply stores. However, if you do bring a dictation recorder, I would recommend using it only as an aid to catch any part of a discussion you didn't quite understand in class. In other words, don't come to class with the dictation recorder and just sit there the whole time thinking that you do not need to pay attention because you have it all recorded. I tried that already and it doesn't work.

Lesson 11 |

Note-taking, The Art of – Part II

Now, let's discuss the layout of your notes. If you had an educational system similar to the one I had, you learned about the Roman numeral outline method early on. You know, with the Roman numerals, capital letters, numbers, and then lower case letters, etc. If that method fits you best, more power to you. However, I have found that system to be too structured for me to be effective, so I will leave you some additional note-taking tips that I have found useful.

1B. <u>Develop your own system.</u>

There is only one best way to take notes, and that is the way that is most comfortable and convenient to you and allows you to remember what was said in class. Don't worry about what others will think of your notes. If you can follow your train of thought, that's what counts. I think everyone would agree that writing from left to right, top to bottom is probably the easiest and most organized way to take notes. But, feel free to use numbers, indentions, and short phrases. Also, feel free to underline, draw arrows connecting pieces of information, draw circles, and make use of stars and bullets to highlight key phrases that make sense to you. By the way, some of these techniques will be tough to do quickly if you are typing your notes on a laptop.

2B. Be consistent.

Whatever your system of numbering, lettering, margin indentions, phrasing, arrows, circles, stars, etc., be consistent. If you use a short phrase to mean something specific, then use that phrase only to mean that particular thought. Or, if you circle items in certain situations, then don't circle items to mean something different. Otherwise, you will only confuse yourself.

3B. Start each class session on a new sheet of paper.

This will help keep you organized. And then, when you re-write your notes (see Point #8B), you can easily tear out the first draft of notes without messing up the previous day's set.

4B. Date each class session.

For instance, if the date is October 11, then up in the left-hand corner write: "10/11." Pretty hi-tech, I know, but this will help you keep track of each day's notes. Also, when your friends come asking you for the notes from Friday, you will have everything right there.

5B. Be somewhat neat and organized.

I say "somewhat" because ideas and information can come rather quickly in the classroom, and if you worry too much about being ultra neat and organized, you will miss a lot of key points. However, you need to be able to read your own writing and follow your train of thought so that, when you sit down to study your notes later, you won't spend needless time trying to figure out what in the world you meant.

6B. Write a bit larger than normal.

This goes with being somewhat neat and organized. When I'm in a hurry, I tend to write smaller and messier. So, if you are like me, writing your notes a little larger than normal can help keep your penmanship readable and save you time in the long run.

7B. Use plenty of space.

As of the time of this printing, the U.S. Government has not rationed the use of paper, so feel free to use what you need. Leave plenty of space between each main idea so you have room to write legibly. If you are writing down a list of things, leave at least one space between each item so you have room to expand on the notes for each item. The key here is to save you time in the long run. If your notes are all scrunched together and in tiny print, you are just creating more work for yourself. Space things out and the notes will be easier to read.

8B. Re-write your notes.

Re-write your notes to make sure they are neat and are in your own words. Expound on any of the concepts that time didn't allow earlier. You might also want to further explain some of your circles and arrows. This procedure is most effective if done within the Window of Recovery, and it accomplishes several things. First, it makes your notes easier to read and follow for future reference. Second, re-writing the concepts in your own words ensures you understand the material. And finally, re-writing the notes helps lock the information into your memory and greatly enhances your recall ability (see Lesson 10 for my opinion on this issue).

For those of you who used a laptop to type your notes in class, you don't really need to worry about neatness. However, re-writing the notes by hand and in your own words will help ensure you understand the material and will help lock the information into your brain (again, please refer to Lesson 10 for some wonderful thoughts on this subject).

9B. <u>Insert notes from reading assignment.</u>

The final step in taking great notes is to insert the margin notes from your reading assignments (see Lesson 15). If you are diligent to write notes in the margins as you read each page, and if you then have the discipline to write those margin notes into your notebook, you should have a very good handle on the entire class up to this point. Then, as you study your notes every day, you will practically memorize everything discussed in every lecture and all the information presented in every reading assignment. You will be extremely prepared for the next test...possibly more than you've ever been.

How to take great notes
Summary:

What to write down

- Things stressed by the professor
  Notes from board or screen, concepts discussed in class

- Write as much as you can

- Put into own words

- Come prepared
  Do reading assignment

- Don't be late

- Get extra help
  Ask professor
  Use dictation recorder

How to write it

- Develop system you'll understand
  Numbers, phrases, underlining, arrows, circles, etc.

- Be consistent

- Start each class with new sheet

- Date each class session

- Be neat and organized

- Write larger than normal

- Use lots of space between notes

- Re-write notes
  Keeps page neat for easier studying
  Can clarify concepts
  Enhances recall

- Insert notes from reading assignment

Lesson 12 |

A Little Note on Notebooks

Since you are going to invest a good deal of time and effort into taking notes, it makes sense to talk a little bit about your notebooks. I would suggest getting a spiral notebook for each class you are taking. That way, you should have enough paper to take lots of notes and you won't feel stingy if you need to tear a piece out every once in a while. Also, I recommend spiral because all of your pages stay together, the pages stay in chronological order, and they are fairly inexpensive. Label the front of each notebook with the name of the corresponding class. That way, it will be easy to pull out the exact notebook you need, instead of taking the time to open it up to see if you have the right one.

I would also recommend having a separate folder. Get the ones that have pockets and three-ring binder capabilities. You may have professors who will distribute hard copies of their lectures or hand out copies of articles that you will not want to throw away or misplace. Since you can't really put them in your spiral notebook, having a folder available is really quite handy. Also, while we're on the subject, buy yourself a three-hole punch and a stapler. If you don't have them, you'll soon find they are like dorm vacuum cleaners. When you need them, nobody seems to have one.

One last thing: Keep a notebook on you at all times. You'll never know when you'll find yourself with a little extra time on your hands. Waiting for class to start? What a great opportunity to review your notes!

Lesson 13 |

Those Odd Moments

As you may recall, **Study Step 2** focuses on studying those notes you took in **Study Step 1**. In order to get through **Study Step 2** quickly and effectively, you will need to make the most of your odd moments.

"Odd Moments" are those weird pockets of time you have throughout the day when nothing is really going on. Take, for instance, those times when you get to class a few minutes early, only to find yourself at your seat waiting for the professor to come in. Or, what about the times you finish eating lunch at 12:30 pm and your next class doesn't start until 1:00 pm? Or, better yet, you may have a class canceled. Wow! You just had about an hour handed to you! These are all times when you have a few extra minutes that you weren't planning on. What do you do with them? If you're like most students, when you arrive early to class, you will either text your friends, or sit awkwardly and wait for class to start, or begin a conversation with the other students in the room. In the case of the thirty minutes between lunch and the "1 o'clock" or in the case of the canceled class, most students will either go to the Student Center and hang out with some of their friends or go back to their room to watch TV, play computer games, or take a quick nap. But, you are not like most students. No matter how small the newly allotted time may seem, you can definitely do something.

Use those odd moments to your advantage. Remember the Window of Recovery? The sooner you can get to those notes, the more solidly those notes will sink into your brain. So, if you are between classes and you can't get to your Study Zone right away, get out your notebook on the way to your next class and start studying. It only takes a few minutes to review the notes from your last class, and those few minutes could make the difference between a "B" and an "A." They could make the difference between staying up late studying and being able to have some fun with your friends later.

I remember going to a home basketball game with some of my friends. As half-time approached, I realized there would be twenty minutes with nothing much going on. So, when the first half ended, I left my friends, went back to my room, got fifteen minutes worth of studying in, and made it back in time for the second half. Leaving my friends at a fun basketball game may not sound very cool, but by taking advantage of my odd moments, I made a 95% or higher in every class that semester and that *was* very cool.

Odd moments will land in your lap more often than you think. So, start looking for them throughout the day and make things happen.

Lesson 14 |

Quiz #1

You're in your last class of the day, and one of your friends leans over to you and says, "Hey, when class gets out, we're going to play cards in the Student Center. You need to come."

What should you do?

See Appendix A for the answer.

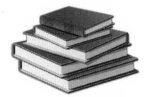

Lesson 15 |

You Are What You Read

Study **Step 3** deals with the mounds of reading you will have, so let's talk about how you can get the most out of your reading in the least amount of time. The faster you can get through the reading material *and* comprehend what you read, the better.

The volume of reading in college can be staggering. It is not uncommon for a professor to say, "Read chapters one through five for next time and be ready for a quiz," or "Read pages 171 – 285 for next class." Now, that may be fine if that were your only class, but you most likely have three or four other classes that are piling on the reading at the same time. You end up with a ton of reading that can seem overwhelming, and if you get behind, it is nearly impossible to catch up. So, just make a point to stay on top of it.

Reading over one hundred pages of your favorite novel each night is one thing, but reading textbook material that may sometimes be dry or difficult to get through is a whole other ball game. Let's face it. You're probably not going to curl up by the fireplace and grab your 11th edition of *Financial and Managerial Accounting* and let yourself escape into the world of debits and credits. Your mind can only absorb so much new information at a time before it begins to wander, and due to the educational nature of textbooks, your mind may go out to right field rather quickly.

So, how can you keep your mind focused and get through all your textbook reading relatively quickly and effectively? I am definitely not a reading pro, but let me give you a few tips that I have found to be effective.

1. Ask yourself questions.

In their classic volume *How to Read a Book*, Mortimer J. Adler and Charles Van Doren stress the importance of asking questions as you read, especially with those books which are expository in nature or nonfiction (like your textbooks). Asking yourself questions while you read gives your mind a task. When your mind has a task, it searches for the answer.[9] Have you ever sat down to read and found yourself reading the same sentence over and over again? Chances are, you didn't put your mind to work and it took a vacation on you somewhere in the previous paragraph. Asking questions forces your mind to focus on what you are reading to come up with the answer.

So, what questions do you need to ask as you read? According to Adler and Van Doren, you need to ask the following four questions in their respective order:

1. What is the book about as a whole?
2. What is being said in detail, and how?
3. Is the book true, in whole or part?
4. What of it?

As your mind seeks to find the answers to these questions, it will stay focused until it finds the answers.[10]

2. Mark up your book.

Adler and Van Doren go on to say that you should mark up your book by underlining major points; star or asterisk the most important points in the book; number the sequence of points; number other pages in the margins that correspond to the same point; circle key phrases; and write notes in the margins that reflect your response, your thought process, or the answers to the four questions you asked yourself when you began reading.[11]

This practice of asking yourself questions, marking up your book, and writing notes in the margins is an acquired skill. It may take a little extra time when you first start, but the more you do it, the quicker and easier it becomes and it can really save you time in the long run.

You may be scared to mark up your book because, if you do, you will not get as much money for it when you sell it back to the bookstore. I know as a college student, every dollar counts. But in this case, the few extra bucks you will get for a clean book are not worth it. Don't shortchange your future! Even if the book is from a class that is not part of your major, get the most out of your class and mark up your book.

3. Use a highlighter sparingly.

Highlighters can be great tools, but if used too much or in the wrong way, they can be a distraction and a hindrance. Have you ever tried to read a textbook, only to find that the previous owner felt the need to highlight nearly the entire page? What's the point? With most of the text highlighted, it is difficult to locate any of the main points. It would have been easier to have a little note at the top of the page saying: "Know this page," or "This page is important." Instead, there are carelessly drawn yellow or pink lines all over the page that are very distracting.

More importantly, highlighters have the potential for laziness. It's tempting to highlight an entire section of text and think, "Now that it stands out, I can easily come back to it later." And so, you put off any mental work until later. You put off forcing your mind to learn the material, and instead, take the easy way out. Or, even worse, you may fool yourself into thinking that if you highlight something, that piece of information will somehow magically get absorbed into your brain and will be locked in.

Highlighters cannot take the place of writing something down. Highlighting does not help you recall the information like writing does. Highlighting only allows you to find information quickly when you come looking for it later. So, never let your highlighter take the place of writing either your thoughts or the answers to your questions. Instead, highlight only the information that supports the main idea and any key information you want to be able to locate at a later time.

4. Re-write margin notes into your notebook.

After you have marked up your book, written the answers to your questions in the margins of your textbook, and highlighted any supporting information, you need to re-write your margin notes into your classroom notebook.

As I mentioned in Lesson 11, there are a few good reasons for doing this seemingly extra step. By writing your margin notes into your classroom notebook, you keep all of your reading and classroom notes together and you incorporate the reading notes into your daily study rotation. That way, you are sure to master all of the material presented in both the classroom discussions and the reading assignments.

5. Watch your daydreaming.

Pay attention to your thoughts. If you find your mind drifting to a galaxy far, far away, and if you have to re-read sentences over and over again, that is a sure sign you are not soaking up what you have just read and it is probably due to two reasons. One cause could be that you are not asking yourself questions as you read, as we discussed back in Point #1. The other reason could be that you are reading too slowly. Your mind is extremely powerful and absorbs more than you realize. If you find yourself reading every word "out loud" in your brain, that may be too slow. Your mind can pick up the image of the text faster than you can say the words, so while you are saying a word in your head, your mind has already processed it and is off in La-La Land waiting for you to catch up. Pick up the pace and force your mind to stay on task.[12] An exception to this rule is when reading technical material. When the information is complicated, I have found that actually vocalizing the words out loud helps my brain piece things together faster than reading silently. Weird, I know, but it works.

If you find yourself falling asleep as you read, you basically have two options. You could either get up and move around frequently or it may be time for a nap.

6. Take short breaks.

When you are reading to learn, you are most likely reading material that is on a higher academic level than where you currently are. Give your brain a break every so often to let it refresh itself and to keep it from going into information overload. I'd say a short, three- to ten-minute break for every forty-five to sixty minutes of reading should be fine. If you are struggling to stay awake, however, take a short break more often.

7. Pretend you are interested.

Some of your textbook reading may not be the least bit exciting to you or even remotely interesting, but you have to get through it somehow. Did you know that if you can simply pretend that you really like it and that the dry book you are reading is really very interesting, you can program your mind to focus and gain the knowledge you are seeking? It's true.[13] Your mind is way cool. So, my final tip is to pretend that the particular subject matter you are studying is extremely exciting and is precisely the information you have been looking for all of your life. And now you have finally found it! Nice. You finally get to learn how to apply accounting measurement and disclosure practices to a variety of contingent and estimated liabilities! Woo-hoo! Call the fam!

....

Lesson 15
Summary:

....

- Ask yourself questions.

- Mark up your book.

- Use a highlighter sparingly.

- Re-write margin notes into your notebook.

- Watch your daydreaming.

- Take short breaks.

- Pretend you are interested.

Lesson 16 |

The Wonderful World of Study Breaks

S tudy breaks are a must. They can do wonders for your studying progress and success, and I encourage you to develop some fun study break traditions of your own. However, there are some parameters to study breaks that you need to be aware of to obtain optimal results. For, if they are not used properly, study breaks can be disastrous to your study routine.

What are study breaks?

Study breaks are periods of time when your mind and body are separated from studying to let your mind relax and "reset" itself before studying again. There are two kinds of study breaks: the Short and the Grande. It is important to know the differences between the two and when to use each one.

The first type of study break is called a Short. As the name implies, it is a short break of three to ten minutes and is used intermittently within long stretches of studying. Since your mind can only effectively handle new information in bite-sized pieces, a Short is an effective tool in allowing your mind to digest the new information properly.

A Grande, on the other hand, is longer, usually lasting anywhere from thirty minutes to two and a half hours. During these periods of time, I recommend that you get completely away from the books and enjoy the company of your friends and have some fun.

Keep in mind that if you faithfully satisfy **The 4 Study Steps** to completion, you are done for the day. You do not have to worry about coming back to study. Once you reach this point, feel free to take all the time you want to do whatever you want. You deserve it.

When should you take study breaks?

Short

You should take a Short several times within long stretches of studying. If the class or project you are working on really intimidates you, I would take a designated Short after only fifteen minutes of work. No matter how difficult the subject matter or assignment, you can at least do it for fifteen minutes. And, since getting started is always the hardest part, you can reward yourself with a break, knowing that you have done something productive. As you progress, start expanding your study time to twenty minutes between study breaks, and then to thirty minutes, and then to forty-five. Pretty soon you'll be studying for an hour straight before needing a rest.

If the material is not super difficult, or if you find yourself able to stay focused, then I suggest taking a designated Short every forty-five to sixty minutes right from the start and not building up to it. If you can handle it, there is no reason to stop. Taking unnecessary breaks will only jeopardize your progress and your success, and you'll run out of time.

Also, pay attention to your thoughts. If you catch yourself starting to daydream, that is probably a good signal that you need a Short. But don't assume that just because your mind goes to wandering, you have to take a break that instant. In fact, it's better if you can hold off for a little bit. Force yourself to hang in there and stick with your studying for just ten more minutes. It is extremely important that you follow through on this point and don't jump ship just because your mind starts spacing out. If you have the fortitude and persistence to stick with it for ten more minutes, amazing things will happen. You will begin to train your mind to remain focused for longer periods of time, and you will feel really good about yourself because you didn't take the easy way out when you wanted to quit. So, hang tough, and don't give in right away to your desire for a break.

If you find it extremely difficult to remain focused for even those ten additional minutes, try increasing your reading speed. For some reason, your mind is off on a tangent and reading at your current pace is slow enough to keep it occupied elsewhere. Pick up the pace and see if that doesn't bring you back into focus.[14]

If you find yourself getting physically tired, you may want to reverse your initial study break routine and start increasing the frequency of your breaks to ensure you stay focused. For example, if it's getting late in the evening and you feel yourself wearing down, take a designated break after thirty minutes, instead of trying to last forty-five to sixty minutes. Then, take another designated break after twenty minutes of studying, and then again after fifteen. That way, you can get another solid hour of studying in without expending your energy trying to stay awake.

Grande

Although a Grande can be rewarding, if not used properly, it can also wreak havoc on your studies and be hazardous to your academic health. Let's examine some important considerations when trying to decide if it's time for a Grande.

First, if you mathematically figure up how much available time you have during the day, you are limited on how many Grandes you can take. Granted, if you take thirty-minute breaks versus two-and-a-half-hour breaks, you could actually fit more in, but you are still limited. Second, when you are away from studying for over thirty minutes at a time, although your mind may be getting a much needed break, you are cutting short your continuity and study momentum. Last, think about the timing. If you take a long break early in the day, before you have gotten much studying done, you are just setting the stage for failure and a day of minimal productivity. With these considerations in mind, I recommend you take at least one Grande per day, but no more than two.

So, when should you take a Grande? Ideally, a Grande should be taken when you are well into **Study Step 3**. The bulk of your study time and energy will most likely be spent doing your reading, so it is here that you will probably need a decent break. I would suggest getting at least half of your reading done before you take a Grande, but you will have to monitor that yourself and determine your particular needs at the time. However, the rule from the above section on the Short still applies: When you feel the need for a break, force yourself to stick with it for ten more minutes before actually taking your break. It will really pay off.

I want to warn you again about the dangers of taking an unnecessary study break. Be truthful with yourself and if you don't need a study break, don't take one just to take one. They will absolutely kill your studying success. So, when you start getting tired, or your friends come by, or you feel like you are missing something special, or a host of other thoughts and distractions that will insist on you taking a break, fight the urge to quit and stick with your studying a little longer. I promise, if you stick with it just a little bit longer, you will feel much better about yourself and you will have more fun going out with your friends once you have successfully completed **The 4 Study Steps**. Otherwise, if you take an early study break, you will always know in the back of your mind that you need to come back to the books later.

Taking unnecessary breaks is like making a bunch of stops on a road trip. Let's say you and a few friends embark on a Spring Break trip that is supposed to take ten hours. However, an hour into the trip, someone has to use the restroom. You stop. Everyone gets out, takes care of business, buys a soda and something to snack on, and then back on the road you go. After a little while, the soda has served its purpose and someone needs to use the restroom again. You stop again. Back on the road again. About an hour later, everyone starts getting hungry. Stop again for lunch. Back on the road. A little while later, you stop to use the restroom...and then again to get some caffeine...and then again to use the restroom. The trip that normally takes about ten hours to complete ends up taking nearly fourteen. Why? Because of all the stops on the trip. The same thing will happen with your studying. If you start taking more and more breaks, it will cost you a lot of time, which will ultimately lead to your study time getting the short end of the stick.

How long should a study break last?

A Short should be no more than ten minutes in length and a Grande should last from thirty minutes to two and a half hours. Be diligent and disciplined with your time, and don't get in the habit of going off on long study break excursions every time your mind gets distracted. If you start allowing your study breaks to run longer than you need, you will end up with the same result as taking more breaks than you need: low productivity.

What should you do on your study breaks?

Short

Get up, get your blood moving, and do something other than study. I don't care what you do, but remove your body from where it has been and do something physical. Walk around, stretch, get something to drink or snack on, do some jumping jacks, get up and turn on some cool music, or use the restroom. Whatever you do, get your body moving. Physical movement and exercise gives your mind renewed energy so it will be able to focus again when you return to the books. Take advantage of your breaks by being a little active and help your brain stay focused for longer periods of time.

Grande

The same instructions in regard to getting up and moving around apply here, but since you have a little more time, your options are greater. A Grande is a good time to go eat a meal, watch a movie with your friends, go to a ball game, etc. But, whatever you do, make sure you get away from studying and let your mind have a rest. These breaks can be quite enjoyable, and I encourage you to develop some fun study break traditions of your own.

Short

- Short break: 3 to 10 minutes.

- Use as needed within long stretches of studying. Try to work up to 45-60 minutes between breaks.

- Take as many as you need.

- Don't get far from your studying, but do some physical activity (e.g. get a drink or snack, do jumping jacks, listen to music, use the restroom).

Grande

- Long break: 30 minutes to 2.5 hours.

- Try to get through most of your reading **(Study Step 3)** before using this break.

- Take one per day; no more than two.

- Get completely away from studying (e.g. eat a meal, watch television, watch a movie, go to a ball game).

Lesson 17 |

The Tortoise and the Hare

This updated classic Aesop fable is a good illustration of what happens when you abuse your study breaks.

The tortoise and the hare were in the same Music Appreciation class in college. After class one day, the hare saw the tortoise trying to read and study the four chapters that were assigned. Noticing that the tortoise was a slow reader, the hare began to make fun of him and say nasty things about his mama. So, the tortoise challenged him to a study duel. Whoever had the higher score on the following day's quiz would be the winner.

The hare, knowing that he was a fast reader and had an easy time in high school, readily accepted the challenge. He immediately started reading and actually made good progress, until he got distracted. He decided he needed a break, so he took a nap and then watched his favorite television shows. He was not concerned, however, because he knew he was a fast reader and could easily read the final three chapters later that evening. Then his friends stopped by and asked if he wanted to go to the concert with them. That sounded like a lot of fun, so he accepted their invitation because, after all, he was a fast reader and he could easily read the final three chapters that night. When the hare returned to his room that night, he was just too tired to read. He was not concerned, however, because he knew he was a fast reader and he could easily read the final three chapters in the morning before class, so he went to bed. The hare overslept, and when he woke up, it was just minutes before quiz time. He hopped off to class, cramming as he went.

The tortoise's day before the quiz was quite different. Knowing that he was a slow reader, he started studying immediately after class and kept plodding along until he completed all four chapters, taking short breaks along the way. Since it was still early in the evening when he finished, he went out and had fun with some of his friends. When he came back to his room that night, he went to bed with confidence, knowing that he was prepared for the upcoming quiz.

The quiz results were no surprise:
Tortoise – 98; Hare – 67.

Lesson 18 |

Quiz #2

It's 4:00 pm on Tuesday afternoon and you're studying in your room. A bunch of your buddies are getting ready to watch a movie down the hall and you get the following text: "Movie n my room. c u n 5."

Will they see you in 5?

See Appendix B for the answer.

Lesson 19 |

Extra Advice on Extra Credit

Several of your classes may have some sort of extra credit assignment you can do to earn a few extra points. It may be doing a little outside reading on a certain topic and writing a short paper on your findings. It may be attending a lecture presented by some world leader, or even watching a certain movie that relates to the class. My Business Law II professor was an ex-marathoner, and he offered extra credit to anyone in the class who beat him in the semi-annual 5K run.

Whenever an extra credit opportunity comes up, do it! The extra effort is usually not that big of a deal, but those extra points could prove very valuable. An extra ten points at the end of the semester may make the difference between a "C" and a "B," or between a "B" and an "A." And, who knows? You may even learn something from the experience.

Although my body ached for several days after barely beating him in the race, having that extra credit from my Business Law II professor felt really, really good. It pushed my overall score in that class up to a 107%!

Lesson 20 |

Are You Smarter Than a 7th Grader?

L et's assume that you have consistently followed through **The 4 Study Steps**, and now it's time to get ready to take an exam. You should be extremely prepared, but here is the litmus test to determine if you really know the material: Can you explain the subject matter of your upcoming test to a seventh grader?

I once had a professor tell me that no matter how well you think you know the material, having the responsibility of explaining that information to another person will force you to learn the material to a greater degree. That's huge, so let me repeat it. No matter how well you think you know the material, having the responsibility of explaining that information to another person will force you to learn the material to a greater degree.

Let me explain. Let's say your Accounting professor has assigned you to give a presentation to the class next Friday. Your topic is the Balance Sheet and how it relates to the Income Statement, the Statement of Retained Earnings, and the Statement of Cash Flows. If you take this assignment seriously, what do you think will happen? You will bust your tail to make sure you know each section of the Balance Sheet extensively. You will also master each section of the Income Statement, the Statement of Retained Earnings, and the Statement of Cash Flows and find out how in the world they tie into each other.

Why will you go to all this trouble? Simply, because as the teacher, you are responsible for explaining to the class how things work and you are under some pressure to deliver. When next Friday comes, do you want to stand up in front of your peers and say, "I'm sorry, but I'm an idiot. I didn't do my work and I really don't know enough about this topic to explain it to you?" I doubt it. To avoid feeling stupid and looking like a dork, you will use this built-in motivation to put in some effort ahead of time and make sure you know what you are talking about.

Remember, no matter how well you think you know the material, having the responsibility of explaining that information to another person will force you to learn the material to a greater degree. As a result of having to stand in front of the class and give your presentation, do you think you will have learned a little more on financial statements? You bet you will. You will probably know more about these financial statements than you ever had before, and you will definitely learn more from this assignment than if you were merely studying to pass a test.

Here's another example. Have you ever tried to give directions to someone? Let's say you are meeting your out-of-town friend at the movie theater. He has no idea how to get there and you are his only navigational system. You've grown up in this town and you know how to get everywhere. You have been to the movie theater several times and have driven past it literally hundreds of times. In fact, you know the route so well you could easily drive to the movie theater without even paying attention. But trying to explain those directions to your friend is a whole different matter. "Well, you go down this street and you turn left. After you turn left, you'll drive for a little bit until you see this house on the left, and then you will turn right. The road will curve a little to the right, but you will go a little further, and then turn left. After you're on this road for a while, you'll turn right at the gas station, and then right again at the bank, and you're there." It's at this point you realize you don't know as much as you thought you did on the subject.

So, what do you do? You're a good friend and you don't want him to get lost, so you find out the actual names of the streets and route numbers and the exact distance until the next turn is required. Here's my point: Even though you know the information (i.e. the directions to the movie theater), having to explain the information to someone else has increased your level of knowledge from simply knowing the information to becoming an authority on the subject.

The same thing will happen with your school work. You have studied diligently and you know the material. But explaining that information to someone else will help you to really know your stuff.

So, why a seventh grader? Why not just explain it to your roommate or to some of your friends? Does it really matter how old they are? Well, you could explain the concepts to another college student, and that would be good, but a seventh grader is special. My professor explained that seventh graders are at that age in which they can hold a decent conversation with you, yet their vocabulary and experience are not as extensive as yours. You can't assume that reciting the information as it is stated in your text, or even as your professor communicated it to you, will suffice. You will need to find a way to break the concepts down to their most basic elements and explain why it works this way and not some other way. You may need to tell the story of the major players involved, how they fit into the picture, and how what they did back in 1651 has changed the way we do things today. Can you see how this would help you learn the information backward and forward?

Now, before we end this lesson, let me tell you that I am *not* suggesting you seek out an actual, real-life, thirteen-year-old and enlighten him or her in the ways of Molecular Biology or American History Since 1877. Instead, the purpose of this little exercise is to get you into teacher mode. Start *pretending* you are always in the presence of seventh graders who are anxiously awaiting the knowledge that you have just studied. Pretend you are responsible for teaching them what they need to know. If you can break the material down and explain it to a seventh grader, you can explain it to anybody. And, once you can do this, you become an authority on the subject and are ready for any exam.

All pretending aside, if you are ever asked to teach a class, do it. You will learn more than you ever thought you would.

Lesson 21 |

Test-taking Made Easy (Yeah, Right).

Basically, you know the material or you don't. And, if you followed **The 4 Study Steps** diligently, you should know the material extremely well. However, when it comes to taking tests, there are some strategies involved that should prove helpful.

First of all, arrive on time or even a little early. There is nothing more stressful than to arrive after the test has already started. So, make sure you are there in plenty of time to free your mind from any unnecessary anxiety.

Also, once you have the test, read the directions for each section carefully. So many students try to jump right in, only to find out they were doing it all wrong to begin with. So, take a few seconds to understand what you are supposed to do.

Next, skim through the entire test. This should take less than a minute. Try to figure out what concepts the professor is trying to test you over and what is worth the most points. Spend the bulk of your time on the weightier questions.

Now, you are ready to begin. Go through and answer the questions you know and skip the ones you don't. When you have finished answering all the questions the first time through, go back to those questions you skipped. Take a few moments to make an educated guess of some sort. If the question is multiple choice, you can usually narrow down the answer to two choices. Again, try to make an educated guess as to the right one. You will probably be right more times than you think. True/False questions can sometimes be the trickiest because, although you have a fifty percent chance of being right, you also have a fifty percent chance of being wrong. One thing to remember is that the entire statement has to be true for the answer to be true. But it only takes one word to make it false.

If it is an essay question, professors will usually give partial credit if an attempt is made that contains some key words or phrases that relate to the question. For example, suppose your Finance test question requires you to help Mr. Smith decide between investing in CDs versus mutual funds, and why. Even if you do not know the correct investment answer to fit Mr. Smith's particular situation, you can at least give an educated guess by stating key phrases like: "It depends on Mr. Smith's 'financial goals' and 'risk tolerance.'" You can also write that, "Although CDs are 'safe investments' with a 'guaranteed rate of return,' the 'tax implications' and 'costs of inflation' on a CD may cost Mr. Smith more than if he would have invested in mutual funds."

When the test is over, immediately look up the answers to the questions that were stumping you. If you missed them on this test, chances are you will be so frustrated with yourself that if those questions come up again on the final, you won't miss them the second time around.

Lesson 21
Summary:

♦ Arrive early.

♦ Read the directions carefully.

♦ Skim through the test and try to find
what is worth the most points.

♦ Answer the questions you know; skip the ones you don't.

♦ If time allows, go back and answer the questions
you previously skipped and make an educated guess.

♦ On an essay question, be sure to include key
words or phrases. Do not leave it blank.

Lesson 22 |

Battle Scars

O kay, so what happens if things didn't go as well as you had hoped? Maybe you didn't grasp the material as well as you wanted, or maybe you didn't do so hot on that last test. Well, you could get super frustrated and discouraged and throw a fit and trash your room. Or, you could learn from your mistakes and see how you could make the most of the situation. I suggest the second option. If you did poorly, you probably realize that just because you are reading this book, your academic struggles will not completely disappear. You also probably realize that you will need more discipline and additional effort to be successful in your quest to get the results that you want.

So, if you did not do as well as you had hoped or if you found that several questions on the test seemed totally new to you, try to figure out where things went wrong. My guess is you did not complete one of **The 4 Study Steps** fully or did not complete it on a consistent basis. Step back and try to identify which area needs work, and then try to complete that step more fully and more consistently from here on. Maybe you didn't do well with **Study Step 1** and didn't take great notes in class. Or, maybe you weren't consistent enough with **Study Step 2** and didn't study each day's set of notes every day. What about your reading assignments? Did you keep up with all of your reading to satisfy **Study Step 3**? And, did you keep up with **Study Step 4** by completing any homework assignments you might have had or by putting some valuable, daily time into an upcoming project? It's the little things done every day that pay big dividends.

Keep in mind, this is about learning. And nothing teaches you more about how to do things right than doing them wrong. Mistakes are your friend, so embrace them. Many successful men and women have gone through the same stressful period of time you are in right now. Most likely, they did not ace every test or finish first in every class. They probably bombed a test or two, forgot to turn in an assignment, and may have even received a low grade in a class. But look where they are now. Take Abraham Lincoln, for example. Did you know he lost the election to the Illinois General Assembly? He lost his job. His business failed. And he was defeated in the election to the U.S. Congress three times before being elected the sixteenth President of the United States.[15] Ultimately, making mistakes or earning low grades is not the end of the world. So, don't give up. You may lose a battle, but don't let it cost you the war.

Lesson 23 |

"Bring It On, Professor. It's Go Time!"

The semester has come to a close and the class is nearly over. There is now only one obstacle that stands between you and the successful completion of the course: Final Exam. Most students are afraid of the final because it is a test of the entire semester. They are afraid because they never truly learned the material the first time. But, again, you are not like most students. You diligently went through **The 4 Study Steps** all semester long, and now it's time to show the professor just exactly what you're made of.

Picture yourself as an entire basketball team that is about to play the most feared team in the country. Every other team is scared to play them because this team is bigger, stronger, and quicker than they are. You are about to play the team that is expected to win. They have had years of dominance over other teams that were awfully good, and based on statistics, your chance of winning doesn't look too promising. However, you are not like the other teams who were defeated. When you step onto the court there is something different. You know every move and every play this team is going to make. You are totally prepared. You paid attention in class and took great notes. By daily going over those notes, you have mastered everything that the professor talked about. However, there were the reading assignments that the professor has the right to pull questions out of, even though they may not have been discussed in class. But, you kept up diligently with the reading, and again, you are prepared. You did every one of your homework assignments and projects, so you will get the deserved credit in those areas as well. So now, when the professor says, "Okay everyone, put your books away," you will look the professor in the eye and say to yourself, "Bring it on, Professor. I'm going to blow this baby out of the water!" And you will.

PRUITT'S COURSE *on* TIME MANAGEMENT

Lesson 24 |

2 to 1

One of the most important aspects to studying at the college level is how you manage your time. Time management is something that you will always need to work on and is something that affects every major area of your life. If you can develop some good habits now, you will prepare yourself for major victories down the road.

Study experts say that a good rule of thumb is to spend at least two hours of outside study time for every one hour of classroom time.[16] Therefore, if you are taking fifteen hours of college credit this semester, you are probably in the classroom about fifteen hours per week. That means you should study at least thirty hours outside the classroom per week. If you are taking sixteen hours, then at least thirty-two hours of outside study time should be planned. You get the idea.

One thing to realize, as you budget your time, is that some of your classes will be harder than others. In this case, you will probably need to spend more than the normal amount of time on those classes. But, your easier classes probably won't need as much effort, so it may balance out.

Lesson 25 |

Balancing the Budget

The first thing you always need to do when you sit down to study is plan your time. Your time is limited and extremely valuable, and, since you want to get the best grades in the classroom and have the most fun outside the classroom, your goal should be to learn the material as quickly and effectively as possible. There are no shortcuts to learning, so you're just going to have to put in the time, which you don't have a lot of.

As I mentioned in the last lesson, you want to try to get at least two hours of outside studying in for every one hour of class time. So, to plan your time, write out **The 4 Study Steps** and write a time deadline for each step.

Study Step 1:

Go to class, pay attention, and take great notes.

Study Step 2:

Go straight to your Study Zone and study your notes immediately, thoroughly, and in order; study all previous days' notes.

Study Step 3:

Do your reading.

Study Step 4:

Complete any homework assignments or work on projects.

Since you are sitting down to study, **Study Step 1** is already done, and now you are trying to maximize your time to complete **Study Steps 2–4** as quickly and effectively as possible. So, after you have written the time deadlines for each step for the day, add up the times and see where you stand.

Here is an example:

Study Notes – :30
Reading – 2:30
Homework/Project – :30

Total – 3:30

In this example, you have determined that you should be able to complete today's studying in three hours and thirty minutes. However, there could be a slight problem. For those of you who have any budgeting experience, you will know that one of the biggest concerns with budgets is that most things cost more than anticipated. Time budgets are no different. What you think should take one hour usually takes an extra thirty minutes or more. What you think should take ten hours usually requires fifteen. So, to accurately assess your time needs, I would recommend budgeting at least fifty percent more time than you think you need. And, if you are a slower reader like me, you'll need more time than that. Therefore, the revised, more realistic time budget would look like this:

Study Notes – :45
Reading – 3:45
Homework/Project – :45

Total – 5:15

Setting a time budget serves at least three purposes. First, it prepares you mentally by giving you an idea of how much overall time you need to allocate to complete your studying. Knowing in advance that you need five hours and fifteen minutes to study will be much better than preparing for three and a half hours and coming up short. It's always better to overestimate your time needs and find you have "extra" time to do other things than it is to underestimate and find you have to squeeze items into an already packed day.

Second, if distractions come up during the day, which they will, having a decent picture in your mind of your time needs enables you to say "No" to the non-urgent things and "Yes" to what really needs to get done (i.e. your studying). You can size up the remainder of your day and see what needs to be moved and adjusted so you can fit in the time you need. I hope you'll realize that starting earlier in the day is much better than waiting until mid- to late afternoon to start studying.

If you find, however, that you simply don't have five hours and fifteen minutes to study, see where you can shave some time off your budget. Can you study your notes in thirty-five minutes, rather than forty-five? Can you read the material in three hours and fifteen minutes, versus three hours and forty-five minutes? I have found that if I know I don't have adequate time to fully complete each of **The 4 Study Steps**, it is better to scale back each step, rather than eliminate a step from your study rotation. This is especially true for **Study Step 4**. It will be easy to cut out **Study Step 4** on those really tight days because you will tell yourself that, since the project isn't due for a few weeks, you've got plenty of time to work on it, but just not today. But, by doing nothing on your project today, it will be easier to put it off again tomorrow. And then, you'll be that much further behind. It won't be long until it reaches the crucial stage, and you'll find yourself scrambling to throw something together. Putting in at least fifteen minutes a day working on your project won't kill you, and you'll be well on your way to completion. So, don't cut this step out.

The third benefit of a time budget is the challenge it immediately poses. If I set aside two hours to get my reading done, I'm going to work hard to make sure I get it done within that time frame, or even sooner, say, one hour and forty-five minutes. With that challenge to beat the clock, I have a focus that is very intense and distractions will be hard pressed to win my attention. But, even in those situations when I don't beat the clock and it takes me three hours to complete the reading assignment instead of two, I can promise that those three hours were extremely productive and have proven a very effective use of my time.

On the other hand, if you start your studying without taking a moment to budget your time, you will have no completion deadline as your goal. Without a completion deadline as your goal, you will be more apt to study aimlessly and deceive yourself into thinking you have more time than you really do. So, you end up spending fifty minutes on a Study Step that you could have completed in twenty.

Start budgeting your time and make it a game. You will find that studying can actually be fun. In fact, budget your time in everything you do, from your professional occupation to your household chores. Try to beat the clock or work on a Dreaded Project for only the amount of time set aside. You will get a lot of things done and you will have more fun doing them.

Lesson 25
Summary:

- ◆ Estimate completion time for **Study Steps 2–4.**

- ◆ Increase estimated times by 50%.

- ◆ Add up individual times to get an overall time budget.

- ◆ Say "No" to the non-urgent things
that come up during the day.

- ◆ Try to beat the clock.

Lesson 26 |

Those Odd Moments Revisited

Now that you have your time budget set, it's time to get after it! You can never get enough encouragement to use your time wisely, so I thought it would be appropriate to bring up those odd moments again. If you can, take a minute to re-read Lesson 13. As you train yourself to keep your eyes open for little pockets of "free" time throughout the day, a whole new world of productivity will open up to you. Start using those odd moments to your advantage, and you will be finished with **The 4 Study Steps** sooner than you thought.

As soon as your first class of the day is over, you're ready to tackle **Study Step 2**, which is to go to your Study Zone and study your day's notes and all previous days' notes immediately. But, most likely, you can't go to your Study Zone because you have another class to go to or some other important function. Not a problem. Start looking for a few minutes here and there to review the notes you just took. Remember, the Window of Recovery only stays open for so long. The sooner you can get to those notes, the longer that information will stay in your conscious mind and the stronger your recall ability will be later.[17]

So, now you're waiting for your second class of the day to start and you've already studied your notes. Good job! Now, go on to **Study Step 3** and start your reading assignment. Even if you only have two minutes and you only get half of a page read, those two minutes were very effectively used.

In fact, I have found that if the reading material is difficult, or more technical in nature, I can gain an understanding faster if I break up the reading into small segments. I have also found that if I spend too much time on difficult or technical material during one sitting, my brain goes into overload and I can't grasp what I am supposed to grasp. I immediately begin daydreaming about other things and it becomes extremely hard to focus. However, if I break the reading down into small segments over and over, my brain is forced to go back to where it left off and reassemble the concept. By continually going back to it again and again, my brain begins to understand the information faster. This strategy of repeat readings is actually supported by several authors in a journal article published in *Psychology in the Schools.* They say that repeated readings can increase a student's accuracy on comprehension.[18] Try it for yourself and see if it works for you.

Remember our five-hour-and-fifteen-minute time budget illustration from the previous lesson? Let's follow the time management techniques of two brothers, A. Student and C. Student, as they studied throughout the day. They both set up a time budget and knew they needed to put in about five hours and fifteen minutes of studying.

A. Student began studying his notes as soon as his first class of the day was over and found that, since he started immediately, it only took him four minutes to master today's notes from his first class. He found several small opportunities throughout the day to continue to study his notes from previous days, and when his final class for the day ended at 1:50 pm, he went right to his Study Zone. Since he had been studying a little here and there throughout the day, it only took him ten additional minutes to complete **Study Step 2**. He jumped right into his reading assignment, and after each forty-five-minute reading segment, he took a short, five- to ten-minute study break. He read up until 5:45 pm, nearly completing **Study Step 3**. He then took a Grande study break and went to eat dinner with his friends. He came back to his reading assignment at 7:45 pm and was finished with **Study Step 3** by 8:30 pm. He then took another ten-minute break before starting **Study Step 4**. Since he didn't have any homework assignment, he spent fifteen minutes working on his research paper that was due in four weeks. It was now nearly 9:00 pm, and he was completely done studying and enjoyed the rest of the evening with his friends.

C. Student did not study his notes at all between classes, and when his final class was over at 1:50 pm, he went to the Student Center to play cards with some friends. At 3:00 pm, he went to his Study Zone in the library and began studying his notes. It had been over six hours since his first class got out, so the Window of Recovery was closed and it took longer to review the notes. In fact, what should have taken him about twenty minutes, ended up taking him forty-five. He then began **Study Step 3** at 3:45 pm. Like his brother, he also took five-to ten-minute study breaks after each forty-five-minute reading segment, but his reading time was cut short to go eat dinner at 5:45 pm with his friends. At 6:30 pm, he returned to his Study Zone and read for another thirty minutes before he left to go to a movie. When he returned to his Study Zone at 10:30 pm, he read for another thirty minutes, but then the library closed. Frustrated, he went back to his room and tried to get some productive reading in. However, he was tired, the dorm was noisy, and he wanted to watch television with his roommate. At 11:45 pm, he gave his reading assignment one more attempt. But, since he had taken so much time off between his readings and because he was tired, he couldn't finish **Study Step 3** in three hours and forty-five minutes. Instead, he gave up at 1:30 am and went to bed exhausted and discouraged. He completed only half of **Study Step 3** and didn't even touch **Study Step 4**.

A. Student

- Used odd moments throughout the day to study notes.

- Went to Study Zone immediately after class.
  Did not let Window of Recovery expire and was
  able to shorten **Study Step 2**.

- Took Short study breaks during **Study Step 3**.

- Took one Grande study break after completing
  most of **Study Step 3**.

- Completed **Study Step 4** in the evening and
  enjoyed time with his friends.

C. Student

- Did not use odd moments throughout the day
  to study notes.

- Went to the Student Center immediately after
  class to play cards and lost his Window of Recovery.
  Study Step 2 took longer than necessary.

- Took Short study breaks during **Study Step 3**.

- Took three Grande study breaks before **Study Step 3**
  was completed.

- Studied past midnight and didn't even finish **Study Step 3**
  or start **Study Step 4**.

Remember, odd moments will land in your lap more often than
you think. Take advantage of them and put yourself ahead of the game.

Lesson 27 |

The Daily Nap

Taking a nap is part of the daily routine for many college students. But *when* you take your nap needs to be strategized.

First of all, don't take a nap during class. We've all done it, but professors hate it and it doesn't do you any good. When you're extremely tired, it's hard to pay attention and take great notes. If you can't take great notes, you mess up the foundation of your study method. So, if you know you're about to drop, get some caffeine before class starts so you won't miss anything the professor says. I can remember being so tired from staying up all night my freshman year, preparing for a Calculus test, that I actually fell asleep in the middle of the test! I woke up several times, only to find pencil marks streaking down the test sheet. Needless to say, that test score was pretty indicative of my success in that class.

Also, hold off on taking your nap until after you have studied your classroom notes. I know this sounds picky, but yes, it matters. If you sleep somewhere between class time and your completion of **Study Step 2**, information will get lost. It always does. The Window of Recovery will automatically close. If you can train yourself to wait and take your nap after you study your notes, you will find that your recall of the classroom material is a lot more effective. So, study first, then sleep.

How long should a nap be? This has been the source of much debate in my house. I think twenty- to thirty-minute naps are the best thing ever, but my wife swears she needs two to three hours of sleep every time. Granted, we have three children all under the age of five, and the two boys are eleven months and eight days apart. So, I guess if I went through what she goes through every day, I'd probably push for two-hour naps too.

However, I have read several articles that say that twenty-minute naps are incredibly powerful for rejuvenating the mind and body and helping them function at their optimal ability.[19] I have also read somewhere that if you can't sleep, but can at least get your body to a relaxed state for twenty minutes, that relaxation is equivalent to four hours of sleep! I'm not sure what the significance of twenty minutes is, but it has been my experience that short, twenty-minute naps have given me a lot of energy for a productive day. However, the times I have napped for an hour or longer usually made me feel groggy, fatigued, and messed up my sleeping schedule. So, if you are one of those who take long naps, try giving the twenty-minute nap a shot and see how you feel. You may not like it at first, but keep at it. I promise that once you train your body to take short naps, you will get a lot more done.

Lesson 27
Summary:

- If you take a nap, take it after you have completed **Study Step 2**.

- Try taking short, twenty- to thirty-minute naps.

- Short naps are great for overall energy and productivity.

Lesson 28 |

Get Up at the Same Time Every Day

This may be one of the most difficult lessons in this book, but since we're on the topic of sleep, let me encourage you to train yourself to get up at the same time every day – even on Saturdays and Sundays. If you get up at 7:00 am during the week, then get in the habit of getting up at 7:00 am on the weekends. This has been one of the best techniques I have found to gain increased productivity, energy, and an overall good attitude, and it is one of the best habits I can recommend. I know you're tired, but get up and do something anyway. If you really need a nap, you can take a short one later.

The only exception I can think of is if you are sick. If you are truly ill, sleep as much as you can to get over being sick as quickly as you can. But, if you are scared to get out of bed, you can trick your mind into thinking you are sick. If this is the case, you are not really ill and you need to get out of bed. You'll feel much better once you're up and doing something.

Getting up at the same time every day is beneficial for several reasons. First, it helps train your body to get up and be more alert when it needs to be. For example, if you are in the habit of getting out of bed at 7:00 am every day, your body will automatically wake up at 7:00 am and be ready to go. Then, instead of dragging yourself to class on a Monday morning and barely able to open your eyes, you'll be fresh and focused and ready to tackle the day. You will be able to concentrate better in your classes and understand more of what's going on.

Getting up at the same time every day also gives you more "awake" hours to get stuff done. By getting up at 7:00 am on a Saturday, for instance, you should be able to get an extra three to four hours of solid studying in before the rest of campus even wakes up. And getting started early in the day will pay big dividends. You will feel extremely productive because you will *be* extremely productive. This sense of accomplishment will fuel your energy to get even more work done throughout the day. As a result, you will really be able to enjoy your Saturday afternoons and evenings with your friends.

Even if you have a late night, force yourself to continue to get up at the same time in the morning. It may be a rough day, but the benefits could be astronomical. Otherwise, if you get up early for five days and then sleep late the other two, your body will have to re-train itself each week to get up at 7:00 am and it won't be as effective. And, if you think about it, Saturday is the ideal day to get up early. Since you don't have any classes, you should be able to take a short nap whenever you need one. What a deal!

By the way, you may be aware that it takes twenty-one consecutive days to firmly establish a good habit. That is true, but it won't take twenty-one days for you to start noticing a huge difference in your energy level. My guess is that after four or five days, you will start to experience a true shift in your sleeping pattern and will have more energy and alertness earlier in the morning. And this goes for all you night people out there. I am a night person by nature, too, and I used to stay up extremely late on a regular basis, mostly because my study habits were so poor. However, my habits have changed, and I am able to have more productive days than ever before.

Of all the successful people I've read about, each one gets up before 6:00 am. Zig Ziglar, one of the most successful salesmen in U.S. history, gets up at 5:30 am each morning to go running.[20] Sam Walton, founder of Wal-Mart, would come into the office every Saturday morning, usually around 2:00 or 3:00 am, to go through the weekly reports.[21] If Sam Walton could get to the office by 3:00 am, you can at least get out of bed by 7:00 am.

Zig Ziglar tells the story of the time he got back late from a trip, and by the time he got to bed, it was 4:00 am. Like every other morning, his "opportunity clock" would sound off at 5:30 am and wake him up to go running. And, on this particular occasion, it would do the same thing…in only ninety minutes.

"Just ninety minutes of sleep? Zig, you can't do that! You need your sleep," he told himself. Any rational human being wouldn't blame him for going back to bed. Any rational person would stay in bed until at least 8:00 or 9:00 am or later. But, even though every fiber in his body wanted to stay in bed, he got up and went running at 5:30 am, just as he did every other morning. He claims that even though he may not have had the most productive day that day, it was one of the best business decisions he ever made. Why? Because something may come up later that would cause him to get to bed late. And, had he slept in one time, it would be much easier to sleep in a second time and a third time.[22] He knew that in order to be successful, he had to get up at the same time every day. What about you?

Lesson 29 |

Ah, Those Wonderful Weekends

Weekends are indeed wonderful for the mind and body, for they allow us to take a much-needed break from our weekly duties. In college, you'll soon realize that, until the semester ends, your work is never really completely done. There is always more you can read, always more you can study, and always more you can work on an upcoming project. So, with all the work that never seems to end, how should the successful student spend his or her weekend?

FRIDAY

Since the weekend really begins when class is dismissed on Friday afternoon, I'll address that day first. Friday afternoons should be no different from other weekday afternoons. Study your notes and do your reading assignments just as you would any other weekday, but only until about 5:00 or 5:30 pm. This should still give you a solid two to three hours of studying for the day, which may be more than most students put in all weekend. Then, you can really enjoy your evening, knowing that you have gotten a lot of your studying done before Friday night.

If you actually have class until 5:00 or 5:30 pm, then spend some time immediately after class completing **Study Step 2** before you call it quits for the evening. Putting in a little study time before the weekend starts will go a long way.

SATURDAY

Every Saturday is a holiday. It ranks right up there with Christmas and New Year's. Nothing, and I mean nothing, usually goes on before noon on a Saturday because most students do not get out of bed until noon on a Saturday. The campus is completely dead during the morning hours. After noon, however, the campus starts to wake up, and it is usually a great time to go to the lake, lay out on the lawn, or go into the big city, and you need to take advantage of those opportunities.

However, Saturday mornings for you should be different than they are for most students. We have already talked about getting up at the same time every day and this is incredibly important. So, now that you're up and while everyone else is sleeping, you should be able to get three to four hours of solid studying in before noon without any interruption. Just follow **The 4 Study Steps** like you normally would. If you're caught up with your reading, you may just want to skim over what you have read to reinforce the concepts. But, most likely, there will be some reading you will need to finish and this is a great time to do it. Once noon comes, the campus will start to come alive and you should go enjoy it without any thought of the books.

SUNDAY

Sunday is very similar to Saturday, and you need to get up at the same time you do during the week. If you followed through diligently with **The 4 Study Steps**, you should be nearly caught up with everything. However, take some time to review all of your notes from the semester. If you still have some reading to catch up on, spend some time on that. But Sunday should be another relaxing day. If you need a nap, take a short one.

Lesson 30 |

Quiz #3

You were up extremely late last night finishing a paper. You just turned in that paper during the final class of the day, and now that all of your classes are done, you just want to go back to your room and unwind. Maybe put on some music, turn on the TV, or take a quick nap. Your body is spent and you need to relax.

What should you do?

See Appendix C for the answer.

Lesson 31 |

Overcoming the Project Blues – Part I

At the beginning of the semester, the professor will usually have a syllabus that outlines the reading assignments for each class period and the dates of the tests. If you look closely toward the end of the semester, there may be these words: **PROJECT DUE**. It may be a twenty-page paper or a group presentation, but the reaction is usually the same: fear and dread.

You should remember that **Study Step 4** is to work on your upcoming projects on a daily basis. If you are like most people, you will put off these projects until the last possible moment. You will live through three-fourths of the semester with this awful dread in the back of your mind that always seems to remind you of your big project coming up. You put off starting the project by making tons of excuses, and fear of the project continues to mount until the deadline is only a few days away. Finally, at this point, you begin the Dreaded Project full of stress and anxiety, and the end result is usually less than stellar.

However, there is a much easier way to tackle the Dreaded Project that can save you lots of stress and help you turn in high-quality work. What's the secret? START NOW!! Don't wait until the last minute. Stop putting it off. Get over your fear by getting started today. Don't slack off on **Study Step 4**, even though it will be easy to rationalize dropping this from your daily schedule. After all, you're busy, and it's hard enough to find adequate time in the day to keep up with your reading assignments. And now, you are expected to work on a project that may not be due for several weeks? Yes. Whatever you do, do something. Put some effort into that project today. If you decide to put it off until tomorrow, that decision will come back to haunt you because it will be easier to put it off again another day, and then another day, and then another day. Have the discipline to stick with it. Simply doing a little bit of a project or job you dread will give you instant confidence and will make it easier to come back to it.

Have you ever seen the movie, *What About Bob?* Bill Murray brilliantly portrays Bob, a character who is afraid of everything. He is scared to get on the bus, scared to get in an elevator, scared to even go outside his apartment. In spite of his fears, he sets an appointment with Dr. Leo Marvin, who teaches him to take "baby steps." Baby steps out of the office. Baby steps down the hall. Baby steps down the street. Those small steps are easy enough, and after a while those little steps add up. By the end of the movie, Bob has been cured of all his horrendous fears by learning to take small baby steps toward his goals.[23] The same principle applies to your Dreaded Project and other things you hate to do.

If you follow through with **Study Step 4** every day, this project won't be nearly as hard as you think. Just tell yourself that you will spend only fifteen solid minutes going to the library or getting online to locate your research materials. That's it. Fifteen minutes. Now, that's pretty easy, isn't it? When the fifteen minutes are up, don't work on the project any more that day. Fifteen minutes won't kill your study or social schedule and you can feel great, knowing that you've completed the hardest part of the project—getting started.

When it comes time to start writing, again, break it down into easy-to-swallow portions. Tell yourself you are only going to write three sentences. That's it. Three sentences should be easy enough. Take a short break, and then come back and write just three more. Then you'll have six sentences, and soon you'll have nine, and before long you may not be able to stop at three because you'll be on a roll. Before you know it, a whole page will be done! Wow! At this rate you will have your whole project completed *before* the due date, and won't that be a nice change?

The Project Blues will hit you several times in your life because you will always have things come up that you really don't want to do. How you deal with these situations will either cause you lots of stress or relieve you of lots of stress. If you can master this lesson, I really think your overall attitude about life will improve. You will have more time to enjoy with the ones you love, and the time spent with them will be much better because you will possess confidence and peace, knowing that you have done your very best.

Lesson 32 |

Overcoming the Project Blues – Part II

L et's expand on this issue a little more. Please note that although **Study Step 4** instructs you to spend a small amount of daily time on an upcoming project, that probably won't cut it. Realistically, those fifteen minutes per day won't be enough to get much accomplished. Sooner or later you will have to devote some larger chunks of time and energy to getting this thing done. **Study Step 4** is only meant to help you get started and to help you stick with it every day. By working on your project every day, your creative juices will begin to flow, and you can finish the project with a much better result.

Here's how I suggest you knock these projects out. As soon as you know the assignment, take time to sort out what you need to do and break the steps down into very small, bite-sized portions (baby steps). Then, assign an amount of time in which you think you should be able to complete each individual step. Simply add up the individual times and you have an overall time budget for this project, just like you did in Lesson 25 on "Balancing the Budget."

After you have set up your time budget, set up deadlines for each individual step. Wherever you keep your calendar or daily planner, write down these individual deadlines so you can see what steps need to be done on what day. Putting the steps on paper will force you to plan your time well and will give you easy success targets.

The following example is a group research project. In this example, the scheduled group presentation is on October 31. Note the small, easy, doable steps that have been set up to be completed early in the semester. If you put off starting the project until later, you are only creating more work for yourself down the road.

Sample schedule for group research project

Fri. Sept. 5	Set up meeting time with other team members
Mon. Sept. 8	Meet with team members; discuss schedule and responsibilities
Wed. Sept. 10	Have list of necessary books and resources compiled
Fri. Sept. 12	Have books or resources in my possession
Fri. Sept. 19	Complete the research from primary book or resource
Mon. Sept. 22	Meet with team to discuss progress and strategy
Fri. Sept. 26	Complete the research from secondary books or resources
Sat. Sept. 27	Write ten to twelve sentences
Sun. Sept. 28	Write ten to twelve sentences
Mon. Sept. 29	Write ten to twelve sentences; complete one page of writing
Wed. Oct. 1	Complete second page of writing and re-write page one
Sat. Oct. 4	Complete third page of writing and re-write pages one and two
Mon. Oct. 6	Meet with team to discuss progress
Wed. Oct. 8	Complete fourth page of writing and re-write pages one through three
Sat. Oct. 11	Complete fifth page of writing and re-write pages one through four
Tues. Oct. 14	Complete sixth page of writing and re-write pages one through five
Fri. Oct. 17	**Final draft finished and complete my portion of presentation**
Wed. Oct. 22	Practice my portion of presentation three times
Thurs. Oct. 23	Meet with team to practice presentation
Tues. Oct. 28	Meet with team to practice presentation
Wed. Oct. 29	Meet with team to practice presentation
Thurs. Oct. 30	Meet with team for final practice
Fri. Oct. 31	**Group Presentation**

One important technique that is extremely effective is to schedule your completion deadline *before* the actual deadline. How far in advance will depend on the magnitude of the project and how much time you have until the actual deadline. For those projects that are bigger, you will most likely have longer to complete them, and therefore, you need to schedule your completion deadline earlier. For example, when it comes to your major papers, your professors will usually let you know well in advance of when they are actually due because they realize it will take considerable effort on your part to turn in the level of product they expect. Therefore, you should try to schedule the completion of these bigger projects anywhere from three days to two weeks in advance. On the other hand, if the project is smaller, your professors probably will not give you as much lead time, and, as a result, you really can't schedule your completion deadline too far in advance. An article summary, for example, could be due the next class period, so your scheduled completion for these smaller projects should be several hours to one day in advance.

Our group project shown above is considered a big project, so note that we have scheduled our completion deadline (Friday, Oct. 17) two weeks before the actual deadline (Friday, Oct. 31). Granted, we still have to practice and polish our presentation, but the research and writing portion is scheduled to be completed well before the actual deadline.

Now, is any of this really possible? Is it even realistic to think you could have your work completed three to fourteen days before the project is actually due? For most students, there is no way. There is no way they will finish even one day ahead of the deadline. Why? Because, under their current mindset, most students do not believe they can finish early and will not even try. It's like their brain tells them they can't complete the project until the night before it is due:

"Complete a project early? You can't do that! You've never been able to complete a project early before, so what makes you think you can do it now? No one else is getting it done ahead of time, and neither will you. You have plenty of time anyway, so go relax and have some fun. Why sacrifice the fun you could be having now by working on this project that isn't due for several weeks?"

And so, most students believe what their brain tells them and they will not start their projects until about one week (I'm being generous here) before it is due. They will set themselves up for failure right from the beginning because they wait until it is nearly too late to accomplish their best work and produce a really good project. For most students, getting the project done even one day early is not a realistic goal at all.

Now, I can hear a lot of you saying, "But I do my best work under pressure." I used to think that way too. In high school, I never knew what it was like to get anything done early. I always waited until the last minute to start, and it was at that point that I would finally do something. I told myself I did my best work under pressure, but the truth was I *only* did my work under pressure. But I have to tell you, it was not my best work. And it won't be your best work either.

So, let's see how you can avoid becoming like most students. If the mental dialog a few paragraphs ago sounds all too familiar to you, you might want to consider a possible change in the way you go about doing things. To do that, let's pretend for a bit. Let's pretend you are like most students who will cram ten to fifteen hours of work into their project to get it done the night before it is due. Let's also pretend that, instead of the project being due tomorrow, it is not actually due until one week from now. Do you think you would have spent all that time and energy this week trying to get a project done that isn't due for another week? Probably not. You probably would have waited until it got closer to the due date to really get going.

Okay, now pretend that the project was actually due last week. What would you have done? My guess is you would have still found a way to get your project done on time. You would have spent those same ten to fifteen hours cramming your work in to get it done just before it was due. The only difference is that your ten to fifteen hours of work would have taken place last week instead of this week.

My point is this: The deadline is not the issue. Rather, it is your *perception* of the deadline that motivates you. If you think you have lots of time available, you will merrily mess around until the deadline is nearly upon you. And then, once it reaches "urgent" status, you will pour yourself into that project until it gets done.

But, what if there was a way to change that? What if you could tell your brain that once the project is assigned it instantly goes into "urgent" status and needs to be started right away? That would be huge! If you could train yourself to get into "urgent" mode immediately and start your project earlier in the process, that would change everything. It would allow you to relax so you could take a step back and see what parts of your project need improvement. Could you re-write a section to make it flow better? Could you add an example or illustration that would make your point easier to follow? When you wait until the last minute, however, you may not have that luxury. Your stress level may be so high that it will be easy to overlook some details that could really make your project impressive. So, start immediately and good things will always happen.

Now, if you are still trying to figure out if completing your project before it is due is really worth the effort, there are some additional benefits you should consider. First, by completing your work early, you allow for mistakes, delays, and technology mishaps to take place. Whether it be computer problems or an unexpected illness or accident, something will always come up that will cause delays. Giving yourself at least a three-day cushion should give you plenty of time to fix the problem(s) and ensure you against most setbacks.

Another bonus to starting early and finishing early is that your other classes won't be forsaken or get bumped from your study schedule. Most students will be so overwhelmed those last two or three days before a deadline that they will spend all of their available time and energy on the big project, while their other classes get no attention whatsoever.

And finally, because of the confidence and energy you have from starting early, you will be able to accomplish a whole lot more than usual. It's amazing what the impact of getting a head start on big projects will have on your overall attitude and productivity in all areas. For that reason alone, it is definitely worth the effort.

How will you approach your next project? I encourage you to overcome your fear by starting small and starting immediately.

Baby steps to the online search catalog. Baby steps reading an article. Baby steps writing three sentences. Baby steps completing this huge, horrible project!

....

Lesson 32
Summary:

....

- ◆ Start immediately.

- ◆ Break job into super-small steps.

- ◆ Assign an amount of time to complete each step.

- ◆ Increase estimated times by 50%.

- ◆ Add up individual times to get an overall time budget.

- ◆ Set deadlines for each step.

- ◆ Keep at it every day.

- ◆ Complete project before actual due date.

Lesson 33 |

How to Write a Paper

You may want to consult a few books on this subject, such as Kate Turabian's *A Manual for Writers of Term Papers, Theses, and Dissertations*, but writing a paper is simple. It only takes five steps:

1. Think
2. Read 1
3. Write
4. Read 2
5. Re-write

That's it. Does that sound too hard? Now, I am assuming you have some experience in the technicalities of most papers. You know, the Introduction, the Body, the Conclusion, and the Bibliography. If you need help in these technical areas, contact your English professor or read some other writing guides. If you are interested in finding ways to manage your time so you can write a good college paper and still have time for a life, then read on.

I have inserted this lesson immediately after "Overcoming the Project Blues" because writing a paper and completing that big class project can be very similar in a few ways. First of all, most big projects involve writing a paper of some sort. Second, both carry an enormity about themselves that evokes fear and dread. The key to overcoming both is the same: Break the big task into small steps and get started immediately.

You probably didn't have to write much in high school, but in college, ten-page papers are commonplace. And quite often, they are longer...much longer. Fear of the paper sets in and you are handicapped from the beginning. If you're like me, it is going to take a while to write a good, comprehensible paper that doesn't sound idiotic. Add to that the research you are going to have to do and you have yourself a Dreaded Project. How you approach this monster will make a world of difference, and I suggest you start as soon as possible.

Let's examine the five "easy" steps to writing a good paper. And, by the way, if you want good grades, you need to turn in good papers.

Think

If you take time to sort out what you need to do, you'll be a lot better off than diving in blindly. The hardest part is usually deciding where to start, so if you take a little time to plan, you can feel good knowing that you have actually started and the stress will immediately dissipate.

Re-read the previous lesson on "Overcoming the Project Blues" if you need to, but the "Think" step includes budgeting your time for this paper by breaking the paper into small, easy-to-do steps.

Read 1

This is when you actually get to the research portion of the paper. It will involve getting online or opening some books. To me, this was the most dreaded part because I used to hate to read, especially about a topic I didn't have much interest in. But, here again, break it down into super small, bite-sized pieces. Read and take notes for fifteen minutes, and then stop. Take a five-minute break, and then do another fifteen minutes. Take another five-minute break and do another fifteen minutes. Before you know it, you'll have an hour of research done and you'll be well on your way.

Write

You have to start somewhere, so pick an easy part of your topic and just start writing. If you are like me and writing comes hard for you, force yourself to spend fifteen minutes writing something. Do not leave your desk until those fifteen minutes are up. Write everything that comes to mind. It doesn't have to make sense or be in the correct order. Just type!

I have also found that when I write, I tend to daydream about anything other than the task at hand. When I notice this starting to happen, I try to type something every thirty seconds. It may be a phrase or just a word, but I focus on typing something every thirty seconds, and that has really been helpful in making my writing time productive. Try it yourself.

If a good idea comes to mind when you're not near your computer, find something to write on and write those thoughts down immediately. Good thoughts and word phrases will hit you out of nowhere, and they need to be recorded. Don't assume that you'll remember them. You won't. Get a napkin or scrounge through the trash if you have to, but find something to write on and do it immediately. When you get back to your computer, add those thoughts to your manuscript.

Something amazing will soon start to happen. The more time you spend actually writing, the sooner your brain will start to assemble your abstract thoughts into actual sentences, and then use those sentences to build readable, flowing, non-stupid paragraphs! Soon, those paragraphs will fit together to communicate a whole section or chapter of your paper. Way to go, Writer!

Remember to save your work often and then back up everything at the end of each writing session. Nothing is worse than spending hours on your paper, only to have a technology glitch delete the whole thing. Professors may not have as much sympathy for you as you think they should. After all, if they let you slide, they have to let everyone slide, and that isn't going to happen. So, just take a few moments to back everything up every time.

Read 2

All this step entails is reading what you have written and coming up with different words and phrases that make your paper easier to follow. It could also mean finding more research material to fill in gaps in the essay.

Re-write

... and re-write and re-write it again. Don't ever expect to write a perfect paper the first time, or even the second, or third, or fourth! Just write what comes to mind, and then revise it again and again and again. Pretty soon, you'll find the right connection and you'll actually be proud of what you've got.

If your school has a Writing Center, take your paper to the tutors there and let them help you with what you've written. The goal of most Writing Centers is to assist you in all stages of your paper. But you'd better swallow your pride, though, because they will most likely find several errors and will offer suggestions on how to make your paper better. So, look them up and get whatever help you need.

In the classic movie *A Christmas Story*, there is a scene where Ralphie writes a paper for his teacher and when he turns it in, he imagines her reading it and thinking it is the best paper ever written. In his fantasy she is brought to tears at its sheer quality and gives him an "A+++++++," while his classmates hoist him upon their shoulders as the hero he has rightfully become.[24] I think we all do this to some degree. However, reality sets in and we find there is always room for much improvement. So, take your paper to the Writing Center tutors and let them help you.

Writing a paper does not have to be hard, but it does have to be done. The key to doing a good job, like everything else, is to start small and start immediately.

Lesson 33
Summary:

- Take time to plan your paper.

- Work on it every day.

- Research the topic for at least fifteen minutes per day.

- Write for at least fifteen minutes per day.

- Re-read the paper.

- Fill any gaps in the paper.

- Re-write the paper again and again.

Lesson 34 |

"I'm on a Low Budget!"

No, this lesson is not about how to get your hands on a little extra cash, but it does address the situation that arises for those students who have to go to work or report to a practice of some kind. Remember, the key to successfully completing **Study Steps 2–4** is to use your odd moments wisely throughout the day and to get to your Study Zone at the first possible opportunity. If you have some other obligation after class, completing **Study Steps 2–4** may be difficult to do. Difficult, but not impossible.

Having a job or practice is going to be a fact of life for a lot of students, and, if you are one of them, this may put a slight kink in your study schedule. You will just need to master the art of the odd moments. If your schedule is such that you have to wait until work is over before you can crack open the books, so be it. But it would be better if you could get a head start on your studying before you even leave for work. To do that, as I have said before, you will need to look for ways to free up little blocks of study time here and there to go over your notes. For instance, can you shave twenty minutes off your lunch break? Is there an hour when you don't have class? Do you really need fifteen minutes to get to class, when you can get there in eight and can spend the other seven going over your notes?

How do you use those odd moments of "free" time that we all have periodically throughout the day? Could you be doing something productive during those times? Hey, four minutes may not sound like much, but as I've mentioned before, you will be surprised at how little time it takes to go over the notes from the class you just got out of. Again, the sooner you can get to those notes and start **Study Step 2**, the easier and faster studying will be.

For you freshmen, let me caution you before you sign up for any job during the school year. That first year away from home is very critical, and I would recommend you get acclimated with the college scene before you jump into any job. Although having a job will force you to have a higher level of discipline, it will also take time away from your studying and can make it more difficult to get involved in school activities. Studies show that those students who work more hours have lower GPAs and tend to drop out of school more than those students who work fewer hours or don't work at all.[25] There are some students who need the money, and there are some who really need the money. If you can somehow make it through that first year without a job, stay unemployed. However, if you must have a job, try to at least wait until you've been there one semester, or try to get a job on campus that will be more sympathetic with your schedule. This will at least give you a chance to make the transition to college life a little easier.

Having a job or practice is a tough route for any student, but it can be done. Hang in there and don't get discouraged. Those odd moments you encounter throughout the day are your friend. Look for them and use them to your advantage. Those small doses of time will add up in a hurry and you will be farther along than you thought possible. Then, when work or practice is over, get to your Study Zone at the first opportunity and go through **Study Steps 2–4**. Make sure you continue to follow **The 4 Study Steps** in order and don't cut out a step. I know it will be tempting to skip a step because time is short. But stick with the plan and hang in there.

Lesson 34
Summary:

- Use odd moments wisely throughout the day.

- Try to complete **Study Step 2** before going
  to work or practice.

- When work or practice is over, go to your Study Zone
  to complete **Study Steps 2–4.**

Lesson 35 |

The Key to Having Fun:
You Control the Socializing

The key to having fun in college and still maintaining good study habits is to do the fun, social activities on *your* terms. In other words, let things happen when you decide to do them, not when everyone else wants you to do them. Since you are trying to deepen your level of learning and get great grades, I seriously recommend you get the majority of your studying done before you go out and socialize. I have found that I have a lot more fun with my friends when I have had a productive day first because it's much harder to enjoy myself when I know I need to be studying. So, have the discipline to not get caught up in any spontaneous activity until most of your studying is done. Then, you can use that activity as a Grande study break.

Being spontaneous with your friends may seem like one of those cute and innocent ways to make fun college memories.

But remember...

Lesson 36 |

Spontaneity Kills!

Lesson 37 |

Quiz #4

It's 2:00 pm on Friday afternoon and the weekend is finally here! Your classes are all done and you've had a great week. You've kept up with **The 4 Study Steps** each day, and now it's time for some fun and much deserved relaxation. You're also excited because you have a big date tonight at 6:00 pm. However, before the date begins, there are a few things that need to get done, one of which is a load of laundry.

What should you do?

See Appendix D for the answer.

Lesson 38 |

"Time" Bombs – Part I
Know the Competition

Two killers of time that you really have to watch out for are Discouragement and Stress. On the surface, it may seem trivial to even talk about Discouragement and Stress in this course on Time Management because they are common emotions that we all experience from time to time and are just a way of life. But, as we examine these destructive emotions a little deeper, I hope you will begin to realize just how dangerous they can really be. In this lesson, we will check out what Discouragement and Stress actually look like. In the next lesson, we will look at ways to combat them.

 DISCOURAGEMENT

According to Dictionary.com, *Discouragement* is defined as: "To deprive of courage, hope, or confidence; dishearten; dispirit."[26] Sounds like a real winner. Discouragement is something that takes away your joy, saps your energy, and robs you of all the necessary ingredients for success, all within a matter of seconds. We've all experienced it. We could be having a great day up to this point, but give us some discouraging or disappointing news, and we are instantly changed. Our day turns awful.

Discouragement is an extremely powerful emotion, and we would all agree that we don't want it to be a part of our lives. But how can we keep it from invading our mind? How can we keep it from wrecking our day? It has been my experience that Discouragement usually occurs because of a negative event that has already taken place. Some examples might include not doing as well as you wanted on a test or assignment, not getting selected to be in the jazz band, getting dumped by your girlfriend, and not getting enough accomplished by the end of the day. These are all events that have already taken place and are in the past. They obviously didn't go the way you wanted, so now you're discouraged about what has happened, and, until you can break free, that event may be the only thing you think about for the next several hours, possibly days.

But, the problem is, you can't afford to spend several hours or days dwelling on the past. Setbacks happen to us all on a daily basis, and how you handle the situation will really make a difference in your immediate future. What is done is done. It cannot be changed. Spending pointless hours agonizing over what has taken place is not going to change the outcome. But it will, in fact, make it even worse. By allowing Discouragement to hang around, you will only ensure that you remain depressed and that you get nothing done. Because you are so focused on what has taken place in the past, you cannot focus on the present and what you could be doing right now. Only when Discouragement is fully conquered can you truly be able to focus on the task at hand and be productive again. It's hard enough to get through the semester without any hindrances, but having your mind weighed down by any amount of discouragement can really cause you trouble. In extreme cases, if it's not dealt with early on, it could lead to depression and serious health issues, not to mention poor grades or even dropping out of school.

HOW DISCOURAGEMENT ATTACKS

I have battles with Discouragement every day, and I have noticed that Discouragement attacks me the most often when I don't get everything done. I start each day with my To Do list in one hand and huge expectations of accomplishment in the other. But do things go the way they're planned? Rarely. Something comes up that I wasn't prepared for, or I get interrupted, or some project takes much longer than I anticipated, or life just happens and I can't finish. But, whatever the case, I don't get it all done and I usually exhibit one of two responses. Either I desperately keep working until bedtime, trying to salvage the day, or I just want to give up and quit.

The first response usually happens when I attempt to cram too much into my waking hours. As long as I still have energy, there is hope; I still have a fighting chance to get more done. But, when it's finally bedtime, Discouragement hits and hits hard. I get frustrated, angry, and annoyed, and all that I actually accomplished that day holds little value because I didn't get it *all* done. I hate going to bed because going to bed means I have to surrender. Going to bed means I failed.

On the other days, when I just want to give up and quit, it's usually because my day started off behind schedule. And once I get too far behind, it's extremely difficult to catch up. On these occasions, I just want to write the day off and start over tomorrow. What's the point of even trying when I know there is no chance for a perfectly successful and productive day?

STRESS

Stress, on the other hand, is a different animal. Where Discouragement is a frustration over something that has already taken place, Stress is a fear of what is about to take place, or more appropriately, a fear of what will *not* take place (i.e. the completion of your assignments). It's a fear of the future in which you can't get it all done. Now, keep in mind, a certain amount of stress is actually beneficial. After all, if everything were easy, you wouldn't stretch, or get better, or grow to your full potential. You need some level of stress and adversity in your life, for it's only through adversity that you gain strength and skill. However, when your mind thinks that the adversity you are facing is too much for you to handle, your level of stress increases until it reaches a breaking point, and then your system shuts down. You instantly become immobilized.[27] This dangerous level of stress is the Stress I am referring to here in this lesson, and it is a destructive enemy of effective time management that needs to be overcome.

HOW STRESS ATTACKS

When I get stressed, it's usually because I sense I may be behind schedule, or there seems to be so much to do that I don't even know where to start. As with Discouragement, I also exhibit two usual responses with Stress. Sometimes I get so worked up that my blood pressure shoots through the roof and I can't think straight. I know I've got tons to do, but I just sit, immobilized, unable to concentrate on a single task. Other times, I get so scared I can't get out of bed. I am afraid to face the day and I become extremely tired. If I could, I'd stay in bed and sleep for hours. I end up not wanting to do anything at all, and that's exactly what happens. Then, I get frustrated at myself for not getting anything done and Discouragement takes over. What was once just a sense of being behind is now a fact.

Lesson 39 |

"Time" Bombs – Part II
How to Beat the Competition

So, how can you combat and defeat these dangerous and destructive emotions of Discouragement and Stress? First, learn to identify them and be aware that you are being attacked. You have a much better chance overcoming them when you realize what's going on. Remember, Discouragement is a frustration over something in the past and Stress is a fear of the future. And, although they may attack from different angles, the result is always the same: low productivity.

There are two key concepts you need to understand. First: You can only control what goes into your mind. You cannot change the past, nor can you control the future. You can only live in the present. If you focus your energy on either the past (Discouragement) or the future (Stress), you become immobilized, and you cannot truly live or be productive in the present.

Second: Discouragement and Stress are just states of emotion; they are not reality. In other words, the thoughts that pass through your mind and the fears you experience under their influence do not have to take place. They are not real. They are only as real as you believe them to be. No matter how bleak things appear, your life is not over; it's not the end of the world. Your mind just gets tricked into believing that those frustrations and fears are real and that your life is ruined because the worst is about to happen. Actually, the adversity you are facing is not too much for you to handle. Really, it's not. Your brain just thinks it is. In fact, your brain gets fooled into believing many things that are not true.[28] For example, do any of these sound familiar? "You're not good enough or smart enough to do well in this class. After all, if you were smart, you wouldn't have bombed that last test. You blew it!" "If you were a good writer, you would have had that paper done a long time ago, and it wouldn't sound so stupid." "Nobody wants to hear your presentation." "There's no way you're going to get all that done before Friday." And on and on it goes. But, once you begin to understand these two concepts, you begin to beat the destructive forces of Discouragement and Stress.

 ## BEATING DISCOURAGEMENT

Most likely, Discouragement and Stress will still get to you, even after you have mentally told yourself their lies are not real. So, you will have to employ additional tactics when you find yourself held in their clutches, unable to function. Now, I'm no psychiatrist, but the best way I've found to combat Discouragement is to ask myself: "What is the worst thing that can happen because of this?" Once I think about the worst possible outcome, and how extremely unlikely it is to occur, I immediately feel better. Next, I try to focus on the positive and remind myself of all the things that went right. For example, when I didn't make the jazz band, I was very discouraged for a while. But, when I considered that the worst possible scenario was probably outright jeering and heckling by the entire student body as I walked to class and being called a "loser" by all the pretty girls, and then realized how this would probably never take place, my discouragement began to disappear. Then, I began to think about all the free time I'd have to study and spend with my friends, now that I didn't have to go to jazz band practice. Soon, my world was right again.

Another way to fight Discouragement is to get enough rest. Fatigue and Discouragement seem to go together, so when you are really tired, be on your guard. I can think of multiple times when I was exhausted and then went through a discouraging situation soon afterward. Had I gotten enough rest the night before, I could have saved myself from a lot of frustration and saved myself a lot of time.

Another tactic is to realize that other successful people have had setback after setback hit them throughout their lives, and yet they overcame. Maybe what I'm facing at this moment is a similar setback to what they went through, and if I am to be successful too, I need to shake off the discouragement and start over with a positive attitude right now.

Additionally, I have found it helpful to take responsibility for my own setbacks.[29] When negative events take place, I ask myself if I had anything to do with how things turned out. If so, I make a "Mistake" note in my journal as to what I did wrong. By actually writing it down, I am less likely to make the same mistake again, which will hopefully save me from future discouragement and future time loss. By the way, one seemingly innocent action that has been listed as a "Mistake" in my journal and has been the cause of many a wrecked day is sleeping in. Nothing puts me behind schedule faster than getting a late start. Things are much more productive and more enjoyable when I get up at the same time every day.

Okay, here's a little exercise for all of you who get discouraged when you don't succeed or you don't complete your To Do list. I have found this exercise to be very successful and I hope it can be rewarding for you as well. Picture whatever project you are working on or subject matter you are trying to master. You should probably know by now that you're most likely not going to get it right the first time, the second, or even the third time. Instead, pretend that whatever project or subject matter you are working on is going to take one hundred hours to complete. Now, instead of wasting a lot of time and energy getting discouraged because you didn't succeed after the tenth hour, you should rejoice and get excited about what you actually *did* accomplish on this past attempt because you are now that much closer to success. Persistence is the key. You don't know at what point success will come, but it *will* come. Will it really take one hundred hours? Possibly. Maybe even more. But maybe even less. It may take another ninety hours, or success may come after the very next one. So, don't give up! When you give up and quit, you are guaranteed to lose. But, when you are persistent and keep trying again and again and again, you become a fighter and set yourself up for success.

 BEATING STRESS

When it comes to combating Stress, the main thing to remember is to stay focused and keep working. As long as you are actively working toward your goal, Stress will have a hard time taking over. Just as freezing temperatures are less likely to freeze running water, Stress will have a hard time freezing your brain and productivity if you are actually doing something.

However, if Stress does overtake you, there are two extremely easy and effective strategies you can utilize to turn the battle around. The only hard part is putting them into action. The first is a series of small steps you can use when you find yourself flooded with all the things that need to get done:

1. Take a deep breath.
2. On paper, prioritize what needs to be done.
3. Focus on doing one thing at a time.

When everything comes crashing in, there is a tendency to get all uptight and not know what to do next. Just relax. Remember, you can only do one thing at a time, so block out your distractions and focus your energy on completing that one thing.

The second strategy comes into play when you fear or dread one particular project. This Dreaded Project gives you anxiety and keeps you from being productive. In this case, all you need to do is complete one task toward its completion. That's it. Just one task. Don't think about the entire project. Just focus on completing one simple task. For example, when you're tired and you know you still need to run two miles, don't think about the entire two miles and how long and awful they will be and how you should probably go back to bed and rest because you didn't get much sleep last night and you don't want to get sick. That could be devastating! Instead, tell yourself to run just one block. And then, when that block is conquered, tell yourself to run another block. Focus on small, doable, bite-sized portions. Put your best effort into completing that one simple task, and you will immediately find additional strength and determination to get back on track. Are you behind in your reading? Read one page. Do you need to start your research for a paper? Spend a simple fifteen minutes online or at the library actually working on it. Are you having trouble understanding a concept? Get help immediately. Don't put it off. Make that one call, or send that one email to your professor, or get help from a trustworthy friend. The longer you wait, the harder it will be to start your project the next time and the higher your stress level will be. So, do something! Once you start the task, you instantly demolish the mental block that is keeping you down.

Discouragement and Stress are two big killers of time. They are dangerous and destructive, but you have the power and the ability to overcome them. Take action and don't let them wreck your day or your semester.

Rap Sheet

Discouragement

- Frustration over something in the past.
- Steals: Joy, Energy, Success.
- Result: Depression, Frustration, Low productivity.

To Combat:

1. Learn to identify Discouragement.
2. Control what goes into your mind.
3. Discouragement is just an emotion;
   it is only real if you allow it to be.
4. Determine worst-case scenario.
5. Focus on the positive.
6. Get adequate rest.
7. Know that others have had setbacks.
8. Take responsibility for your setbacks.
9. The Exercise: Be persistent.

Stress

- Worry about the future/not getting everything done.
- Gives: Fear, High anxiety.
- Result: Immobilization, Low productivity.

To Combat:

1. Learn to identify Stress.
2. Control what goes into your mind.
3. Stress is just an emotion;
   it is only real if you allow it to be.
4. Stay focused and keep working.
5. Take a deep breath.
6. Prioritize what needs to be done.
7. Focus on doing one thing at a time.
8. Do one simple task toward the completion
   of the project.

Lesson 40 |

The 15-Minute Drill

A s you have probably noticed, I am a big fan of fifteen-minute time segments, which I call the 15-Minute Drill. The 15-Minute Drill serves three purposes:

1. It breaks any huge project into small, easy-to-accomplish, bite-sized pieces.

I figure that no matter how awful the assignment or task, I can at least do fifteen minutes worth. Getting started is always the hardest part, so if I will work on the Dreaded Project for just fifteen minutes, I can feel good about getting started and keep Discouragement and Stress from setting in. Soon, those fifteen-minute sessions turn into twenty minutes, then thirty minutes, then forty-five minutes, and voila! The Dreaded Project is done, and done well.

2. It serves as a reset button to your brain, producing both clarity of thought and deepened understanding.

I used to give drum set lessons and I would tell my students that if they would only practice forty-five minutes a day, they could be a good drummer. If they took those same forty-five minutes, and split them into three fifteen-minute sessions with a short, five-minute break in between, they could become an excellent drummer. Why? Even though it is the same amount of practice time, I have found that when I give my mind and body a short break, my mind and body have "reset" and everything seems to click when I return. So, when you are trying to master a difficult subject matter, whether it be a certain percussion rhythm, chemistry experiment, or even writing a paper, if you give yourself a short break between fifteen-minute sessions, you'll be amazed at how your mind seems to pull everything together.[30]

3. It serves as an instant jumpstart to productivity.

I once read somewhere that the truly successful people not only set long range goals of twenty years or longer, but they also set goals for the next fifteen minutes. When you want to be successful, you do what the successful people do, so I thought I'd give it a try. Oh, my word! The catch phrase should not be, "What a difference a day makes," but, "What a difference fifteen minutes makes!"

The 15-Minute Drill is a game I constantly play. I tell myself that my goal is to get a certain task done in the next fifteen minutes. And then, boom! I get after it. If I succeed, great; if not, I'm not worried because I am working my tail off and have another fifteen minutes to try again and give it another shot. Try it with your studying, try it at work, and try it at home with your chores around the house. It doesn't matter how lousy a day I've had or how little I've gotten done up until that point. When I play the 15-Minute Drill, I instantly get rejuvenated, get motivated, and get things done.

What are you going to accomplish
in the next fifteen minutes?

The world is waiting to find out.

Lesson 41 |

Jar of Rocks

I'm not sure where I read the following story, but it is an illustration I will never forget. Although the author is unknown and several variations exist, I hope the message will have the same powerful effect on you as it did on me.

Jar of Rocks
Author Unknown

A professor stood at the front of the classroom with a large, empty glass jar. On the table were several large rocks. He gently placed each rock inside the jar until no more rocks could fit. He then asked the class, "Is the jar full?"

"Yes," they exclaimed. "You can't fit any more rocks in there."

He then reached into the cabinet below and set a bowl full of small pebbles on the table. He scooped all the small pebbles into his hands and let them fall into the jar until they reached the top. "Is the jar full?" No one answered.

The professor reached into the cabinet again and produced a bowl full of sand. He poured the sand into the jar and it sifted to all the empty crevices of the jar. He filled it to the brim. Then, he pulled out a pitcher of water and poured the water into the jar until it reached the very top. "Now, the jar is full," he said to the class. "Had we started with the water, the sand, or the pebbles, we may have been able to fit them completely into the jar, but we certainly could not have fit in the rocks.

"Your life is the same way. If you fill your time with small, meaningless activities, you won't have room for the important things. However, if you concentrate on the important things first, you will find that your life will be truly full."

How are you spending your precious time? Start taking inventory of how you spend it, and it will amaze you how much of it is spent on minor activities. Those activities may be important, but are they the most important? Could it be that you are afraid of the main task at hand? Sometimes, when I am faced with a Dreaded Project, I can make all kinds of excuses and find many reasons why I shouldn't do the main job that needs to get done. For example, as I write this section, my wife and kids are spending two weeks in Texas with my in-laws. I have the house to myself and my time is my own. I virtually have no distractions and can do what I want, when I want. Sounds like a writer's dream. However, in moments of fear and dread, I found that instead of sitting down to write, what I really needed to do was fold a load of laundry and clean the house before I got started. After all, wouldn't I be able to think more clearly with a clean house? Before I knew it, the evening was gone and so was my best opportunity to write. Had I at least spent fifteen minutes writing first, I would have been much better off.

Think of studying as placing the large rocks in your jar, and schedule the rest of your activities around it. When you find a good stopping point, take a break and do something else that needs to get done, such as laundry or cleaning. These are important things to do, but not the most important. Keep studying as your set of large rocks, and you'll soon find your jar full of pebbles, sand, and water as well.

PRUITT'S COURSE
on COLLEGE LIFE

Lesson 42 |

"Is This Going to Be on the Test?"

As we discuss college life, let me ask you some questions. What is truly important to you? What is it that twenty years from now will hold the most value to you? Let me suggest that the weightier matters are the relationships you develop, the experiences you have, and the growth you obtain as an individual. These are the more important areas of your life that you need to develop before you graduate from college.

College is an experience that is more than just sitting through a bunch of lectures, taking a few tests, and receiving your degree. It is an education in life. Your college years should teach you how to develop values and ideals of your own, how to react to different situations now that your family isn't around, how to relate and communicate well with others, and how to budget your time and money. College life should mature you so that, at the end of these years, you will be better able to live on your own and function as an adult. The most important determinant of your overall success will be your level of development in these areas.

When I was in college, I made "A's" in many of my classes, but my GPA is not what I cherish most about my college experience. When I first arrived on campus, I knew very few people. But that first semester, I met Troy in my Calculus class and he introduced me to a few of his new friends who lived down the hall. It wasn't long before Troy, Wade, Brent, Tommy, Scott, Russ, Stephen, and I were doing all kinds of things together. A month earlier we had no idea each other even existed. But living in the same dorm and having the experiences we did gave me friendships that will last the rest of my life. I had a great high school experience, but I can easily say that the friendships I made and the experiences I had in college were a lot more meaningful and a lot more fun than those at the prep level. Twenty years after you graduate from college, these will be the things you remember and cherish the most.

That being said, college is also about getting an academic education to open doors for your future. How well you perform in the classroom *is* important because it will help determine how many times you get your foot in the office of prospective employers or graduate schools. Employers and graduate schools are attracted to sharp, competent graduates, and one way to gauge a graduate's ability is to look at the level of his or her grades. Good grades will show anyone interviewing you that you are teachable and have the aptitude and the desire to learn. It is a very competitive world out there, and anything you can do to set yourself apart will definitely help your cause.

It is going to be difficult to truly feel good about your college years if your grades are lower than they need to be. On the flip side, your college years will be empty if you spend so much time studying that you miss out on the college experience that will pass you by. So, in order for you to make the most of your college experience and your valuable time, you need to come in with a game plan. I have been on a college campus for over fifteen years, and I have witnessed thousands of students come to school very excited with anticipation as to what the future holds. A new and exciting chapter in their life is about to begin and most don't have a clue as to what is going on. And, the sad thing is, most don't care. Most students want to get by with as little work as possible. They want to be successful without putting forth their best effort. They want to make the grade without putting in the time. "Is this going to be on the test?" they ask, which translates: "Please don't give me more information than I need or challenge me beyond the bare minimum of what is required of me because I am lazy, and I don't want to do more than I have to." If you are trying to get by with as little work as possible, you won't be successful...period. But when you give your best effort, both in your relationships and in the classroom, great things will happen...guaranteed.

Lesson 43 |

Come With a Game Plan

As I mentioned in the previous lesson, in order for you to make the most of your college experience and your valuable time, you need to come in with a game plan. Decide now what kind of grades you want and convince yourself you are going to do whatever it takes to make that happen. However, I want to encourage you not to limit your game plan to just your GPA. Instead, determine what you want your entire college experience to be like. What do you want to get out of college? What kind of person do you want to be by the time graduation rolls around? Obviously, you want good grades or you wouldn't be reading this book. But go deeper. What is it that you truly want out of the next four or five years of your life?

Basically, what you are trying to determine is two-fold:

1. What type of person do you want to become by graduation date?

2. What experiences do you want to accomplish during your college years?

If you are like most students, you probably want to be a better person four years from now than you are presently. You want to be more mature in most areas of your life than you are right now. But, since it is difficult to measure growth in character traits, I recommend you follow the advice of years of psychology experience and do what the experts say: Picture firmly in your mind the type of person you've always wanted to be. Who is that person? What character traits does that dream person have?[31]

And, what about the so-called "ultimate college experience?" Everyone wants one, but what does that entail? How can *you* have one? We will delve into these questions in the next two lessons, but for now, re-read the two questions that were asked a few paragraphs ago. If we state the two questions differently, we can determine a goal for your college career. That goal is as follows:

BECOME THE PERSON
YOU'VE ALWAYS WANTED TO BE

– AND –

HAVE THE ULTIMATE COLLEGE EXPERIENCE.

This may be going a little deeper than what you initially bargained for. You were just trying to improve your grades, and instead, you're getting a lesson on improving your whole lifestyle! But stay with me. Getting great grades is definitely a part of the "Becoming the person you've always wanted to be and having the ultimate college experience" goal you just established. After all, wouldn't you rather be a person who achieves high grades versus low grades? And, don't you think that achieving great grades will give you a better outlook on life and remove quite a bit of stress and discouragement, which will enable you to enjoy your college years a lot more? You bet it will.

Now, let's talk a little more about your game plan. Your college game plan needs to include steps on how to accomplish the above-mentioned goal. In the next two lessons, you will find the "Pruitt Game Plan" to get you started. The sooner and more completely you can master these lessons, the sooner and more completely you can truly enjoy your college experience.

Lesson 44 |

The "Pruitt Game Plan" – Part I
Become the Person You've
Always Wanted To Be

Let's tackle the first part of your goal and talk about the person you've always wanted to be. Going to college is an opportunity to get a fresh, new start on life, and rarely will you have an opportunity quite like this ever again. If you are human, you have areas in your life that need improvement. Whether it's more discipline to do the good things or wisdom to stop doing the bad things, we all could do better. And one of the neat things about going to college is that when you get there, very few people know you or your past. You get the chance to start over.

Were your grades in high school lower than you desired? Do you regret not getting involved in more extra-curricular activities? Were you scared to try new things or worried about what other people thought of you? Were you intimidated by certain peers or certain events such as speaking in front of a crowd? Do you want to change your image? Take heart, because high school is over and it's time to take things to the next level.

Most of you have probably heard of a To Do list that a lot of people keep, reminding them of the things they want to get done. Not only do I suggest you develop and keep up with your own To Do list, but I recommend you also develop an offshoot of the To Do list and formulate an "I am" list. Instead of keeping track of *things* to accomplish, it is a list of character *traits* to accomplish. It is a list of character traits that you would like to see exemplified in your life. Basically, it is the person you've always wanted to be. Now, since this may be new to you and since you may be short on time, I have included my own "I am" list to get you started. If you are like most students, you will find a large percentage of the characteristics from the following list to be traits you'd like to possess, but feel free to add to it.

I am:

A LEADER ... BY SERVING OTHERS

CARING CONFIDENT BRAVE

CONTENT DECISIVE

DISCIPLINED

ENERGETIC ENTHUSIASTIC

FAITHFUL FOCUSED FORGIVING

FUN GENEROUS GENTLE GOOD

GOOD COMMUNICATOR

GOOD FRIEND GRATEFUL GREAT STUDENT

HEALTHY HONEST INTELLIGENT

JOYFUL KIND LOVING

LOYAL ON TIME OPTIMISTIC

ORGANIZED PATIENT

PEACEFUL PERSISTENT PURE

RELAXED RESPONSIBLE

SELF-CONTROLLED SELFLESS SUBMISSIVE

TRUSTWORTHY UNIQUE

"But I want to be popular!" you say, "And this 'I am' list sounds very old-school!" Start getting the reputation for being responsible, caring, honest, and trustworthy, and don't be surprised when you're asked to head up several organizations...and asked out by those of the opposite gender.

Now, you may still be wondering how a list of character traits fits into a book about studying at the college level. The answer is simply this: These character traits promote Excellence in the way you live, both in your thoughts and in your actions. You should strive to exemplify Excellence in every area of your life—in the way you treat yourself and in the way you treat others. Excellence should permeate every activity of your life, including the work you perform in the classroom.

I hope you noticed that being a "Great Student" is included in the above "I am" list. Start being a great student now. You don't have to wait until next semester; you can start today. Pay attention and take great notes in class *today*. Study those notes on a *daily* basis. Keep up with your reading *today*. Work *daily* on your homework or upcoming projects. Make Excellence your standard in the classroom, and it will start to spill over into other areas of your life as well.

Be the person you've always wanted to be ... today!

Lesson 45 |

The "Pruitt Game Plan" – Part II
Have the UCE

N ow, it is time to address the second part of your goal: Have the ultimate college experience (UCE). What exactly is the UCE? And, what steps can you take to ensure that you have one?

In my opinion, the ultimate college experience consists of three components:

1. **The relationships you develop**
2. **The events you experience and enjoy**
3. **The individual growth you undergo**

I believe these three components are inter-related. The more events you share with other people and the more time you spend with them, the deeper the relationships you will have with them. And every time you get out of your comfort zone to deepen your relationships or experience a new event, you grow as a person.

What creates the UCE will vary with each individual. What one person finds exciting and enjoyable, another person will consider boring. Some people will want to meet every student and go out at every opportunity. Others will prefer hanging out with just a few friends or watching movies together in their dorm room. Whatever your personality, college life will abound with many opportunities for enjoyment.

I'm sure each of you, no matter what your personality, will not find it hard to have fun in college because college life is stinkin' fun! The problem will be saying "No" to the many opportunities for fun and hitting the books instead. I'm not against having a good time. In fact, I want you to be able to look back on your college experience with warm memories, but you need to realize there is the possibility of having too much fun. I'm sure you've heard countless stories of students who had too much fun their freshman year and were suspended from school because their grades were too low or for other reasons. This should not be your story.

So, what should your story be? Well, what do you want it to be? Take several days to think about this. Take several weeks if you have to, but do put some effort into this and consider what you want out of your college years. These ideas will help formulate the game plan for you to get the most out of your college experience. To further assist you with your game plan, I have laid out some suggestions.

My first suggestion is to develop a To Do list. This To Do list will help you establish Excellence in the way you live. Having Excellence as your standard will help deepen your relationships with other people and will improve your overall attitude on life, no matter where you are, no matter what your situation. I have listed a few things to get you started, but please feel free to add some more.

To Do:

1. Ask questions, even if I am afraid of looking stupid.

2. Be a true friend to those who come into my life.

3. Be the first to say hello and greet people by name, not "Hey, Man!" (And if you can't remember names, swallow your pride and ask!)

4. Build quality (not necessarily quantity) relationships.

5. Do my very best in every situation (including studying).

6. Every so often take a different route.

7. Every so often visit a cemetery. (Sounds creepy, but you will be amazed at how things will get put into proper perspective and how fortunate you really are.)

8. Exercise regularly.

9. Genuinely compliment other people.

10. Get involved in leadership opportunities, even if I feel I am not the most qualified.

11. Get involved in the situation, organization, or assignment.

12. Get out of my comfort zone.

13. Improve my oral and written communication skills.

14. Meet new people.

15. Say "No" to requests and events that don't match up with my goals and values.

16. Take the opportunity to visit new places.

My second suggestion is to fill out a "To Experience" list.

To Experience:

1. List traditions of your school.

2. List other things you want to accomplish or get involved in.

The "To Experience" list calls for a little research and effort on your part. To fill out the "To Experience" list, you need to write down the traditions at your school and prioritize them. What is a "must do" and what is a "would-love-to-but-don't-have-to do?" Keep this list someplace where you can refer to it every so often. In fact, it may be nice to keep a journal of your college experiences and write an entry when you do something new, or really fun, or meet someone interesting. During your senior year, it will be neat to look back on all the things you have done. You won't be able to do everything, but if start your college years with a game plan, you'll be surprised at all the things you will have experienced.

Don't know what the "must do's" are at your school? Find a few reputable upperclassmen (or your friendly Admissions Adviser) and ask them what needs to be experienced. They'll be happy to tell you and you may have just found some new friends. Is there a certain restaurant or coffee shop nearby that you just have to go to? What about sporting events, hang-out spots, or movie theaters? Should you join a fraternity, sorority, or social club? Is there a particularly awesome Speech teacher that you need to get?

Now, you may want to do more than just the school traditions. You may want to make your own traditions and do your own thing. The second part of the "To Experience" list is where you can list those entries. Having the UCE may mean making a road trip, going to the lake, or joining the school chorus. It may mean serving as Treasurer for the Psychology club or serving food to homeless people. Whatever you decide to do, give it your very best effort and immerse yourself in the activity.

As you compile your list of things to experience, prioritize them and try to do as many of these as you can before graduation comes. Your valuable time is at stake. By knowing what you want to experience ahead of time, you will save yourself from doing a lot of useless and stupid things and getting caught up in a lot of time-wasting activities.

Believe me. There are plenty of time-wasting activities around campus. But, by saying "No" to these useless activities, you have just freed up more time to enjoy your college experience...and to study. Way to go!

Let me point out here that deepening your level of learning and achieving great grades in the classroom will also add so much more to your college experience. You will have done your best, and that in itself will give you the peace of mind to enjoy the rest of your experience. Besides that, your family won't be nagging you to study more, and won't that be nice?! Instead, they will be so proud of you for your fine work that they may even send you a care package! And getting a care package from your family will always make your day.

Now, I can hear a lot of you saying, "This is ridiculous! I am not going to follow Mark's silly suggestions, and I'm not going to write these things down." I realize these suggestions may sound rather hokey to some, but studies have shown that if you take the time to write your goals down and put a completion date by each one, you are far more likely to actually complete them, as compared to when you merely think about your goals every so often.[32] I really want you to have the absolute best college experience possible, and I know these things work. So, give it a shot, and start making your game plan for the ultimate college experience work for you.

Lesson 46 |

Some Do's...

I know I've given you lots of suggestions in this book, but here are a few more that can really prove to be helpful in your college career.

1. Sleep well.

There are two big reasons to sleep well: your physical health and your academic health.[33] It's hard enough to keep up with the school work when you're healthy, but if you get sick, it compounds the problem. You'll miss classes, you'll miss assignments, and you probably won't keep up with your reading. You won't feel like doing a single thing, and the next thing you know, you'll be extremely behind. After a week or so, your illness may pass and you may physically recover, but your grades that semester probably won't.

Your academic health will also be affected by not being able to focus in class, and a lack of sleep is a sure way to lose that focus. Remember when you thought that staying up until midnight was the coolest thing? In college, you will find that if you can ever get to bed by midnight it will be a pretty cool thing. There is so much going on in the dorms and so many people to see and talk to at night that it's difficult to get to bed at a reasonable hour. Staying up late is just a way of life on campus, but it doesn't have to be super late.

I recommend getting six to eight hours of sleep every night. That should give you enough time to socialize, have some fun, and get any last-minute studying done before calling it quits. I'm confident that if you will be diligent about getting to your Study Zone immediately after class and using your odd moments wisely throughout the day, you'll be able to watch *Sports Center* or your favorite television show with your friends and truly enjoy the evening hours, while still getting a decent amount of sleep.

2. Eat well.

This does not mean eat a lot. You may have heard of the "Freshman Fifteen," and you don't really want that. What you do want, though, is to eat healthy foods and drink plenty of fluids such as water and juice. Get in the habit of eating plenty of vegetables and fruit every day. If you think the college cafeteria is awful and doesn't even carry healthy food, you need to look a little harder. Good fruits and veggies and plenty of water every day will help your body and mind function the way they were designed.[34]

3. Exercise.

You may think you are so busy that you don't have time to exercise. However, by exercising regularly you should be able to add more productive hours to your day.[35] In addition, studies show a positive correlation between exercise and brain cognition. In other words, with regular exercise, your brain will understand more of what you are trying to study.[36] You'll sleep better, you'll wake up with more energy, you'll focus better, and you'll feel tons better about yourself. So, even if it's a short, fifteen-minute walk, do it. Your body needs to get the blood flowing to your brain, and the best way to do that is to get off your duff and do some physical activity such as walking, running, biking, or swimming. You may even want to get some of your friends and go exercise together. But, whatever type of exercise you like to do, do it consistently.

4. Get involved.

College is so much more than going to class and getting a formal education. Take advantage of the many opportunities that abound and get involved. Get out of your dorm room and meet the students down the hall. Consider joining an organization on campus, such as a fraternity, sorority, or social club. I have known many students who were afraid to get out of their comfort zone and it cost them a large part of their could-have-been college experience. Now, before you sign up, you need to count the cost of each opportunity and determine if you can really handle the time and commitment it's going to take. You don't want your education to suffer, but you need to get involved.

Lesson 47 |

Some Don'ts...

O n the other hand, here are some additional things to consider.

1. Don't skip class.

The more time you spend away from your goals, the harder it will be to successfully complete them. The same thing applies to your classes. Even if your class does not have an attendance policy, you can't expect to learn the material and keep up if you are absent. Also, if you have a professor who seems to lecture straight from the book and you feel you could use your time more efficiently doing other things, stick it out by going to class and paying attention. By listening and taking great notes, you will greatly reduce your study time because the teacher is reinforcing what you have already read. The more times you hear it, the stronger it is locked in your brain.[37] Besides, it usually happens that when you think the professor is just going to repeat the book again, he or she will present some vital information that you will not want to miss or will give a pop quiz.

You will also find that when spring comes and the weather starts warming up, a lot of your friends will want to skip class to go to the lake. Don't do it. Instead, go to the lake on Saturday. Once you skip class, you are inviting low grades to be a part of your life.

2. Don't rely on your friends' notes.

Most students aren't going to have the same level of discipline as you, and the way they pay attention in class and take notes is going to reflect that. So, if you happen to miss class for some reason, go directly to the professor first to get the notes. If that proves unsuccessful, choose someone in the class who you know is sharp enough to take decent notes and ask him or her. Even if you don't know the person very well, most students are fairly congenial and are willing to help out.

3. Don't assume you are going to remember key information.

Write it down.

4. Don't study with a group.

This suggestion may raise some eyebrows, but my experience with study groups has been more social than academic. At the end of each study group session, I rarely felt like I had accomplished a whole lot and I probably could have gotten more done had I spent that hour studying the material myself, rather than gabbing with the other students.

So, be honest with yourself. If a study group really helps you learn the material, go for it. If you find, however, that your study group spends more time on what happened last night on TV or on the latest campus breakup, then either find someone who can help you one-on-one or go it alone.

5. Don't be afraid to take hard classes.

Organic Chemistry, Anatomy & Physiology, Intermediate Accounting. Tough classes may challenge you more than you signed up for, but the accomplishment can enhance your academic and professional career more than you may ever know.[38]

6. Don't cheat.

Cheaters will never win. Never. Cheating does you absolutely no good, and the consequences far outweigh the moment of "success." If you study the way I've suggested, there is no need to cheat.

7. Don't plagiarize.

Plagiarism is a form of cheating, so re-read Point #6. Learn to write your own stuff.

8. Don't do to others what you would not want them to do to you.

This philosophy is the flip side of the Golden Rule and has kept me out of a lot of trouble.

9. Don't spread yourself too thin.

There are many good activities and organizations to take part in, but you are going to have to learn to say "No" to several of these opportunities that come your way. It is necessary to get involved, but you need to limit your activities. Every activity and organization that you are committed to bites into your study time, which then chews up whatever time you were going to spend with your friends.

10. Don't start dating your first week of school.

Actually, I'd steer clear of a relationship for the entire first semester. Give yourself time to get to know what it's like to be in college. Give yourself time to get into a study routine. Having a girlfriend or boyfriend too early can really put a pinch on your time and your college experience.

11. Don't leave your book bag, computer, or umbrella unattended.

12. Don't get behind.

Lesson 48 |

Don't Cheat!

What do Martha Stewart, Bernard Madoff, and Barry Bonds all have in common? They all cheated. Two of them have received jail time for their cheating, and the other should have an asterisk by his name in the record books with the footnote: *Cheated to break the record.

I want to take a moment to expand a little bit on Point #6 from Lesson 47. There is a lot of emphasis placed on getting a high GPA, and it is coming at the expense of moral character and actually learning the material. In a survey conducted among college students, a full seventy-eight percent admitted to cheating.[39] In another survey, when questioned why they cheated, students revealed that they felt everyone cheated and that companies and graduate schools gave preference to those with high GPAs.[40] So, since there is a slim chance of getting caught, most students will do whatever it takes to get high scores, including looking up answers, copying other people's work, or having someone else complete the assignment.

However, colleges and universities are getting better at catching students when they cheat. For example, professors used to have a hard time proving whether or not a student committed plagiarism. They basically had to rely on their best judgment, and since it was difficult to prove anything, professors usually would not contest it. However, they now have computer programs at their disposal that are quick, accurate, and very effective at detecting plagiarism.

Also, colleges and universities are handing down stiff penalties. If a student gets caught cheating or plagiarizing, most schools will give an automatic "F" in the class and/or suspend the student from school. A professor friend of mine told me about one of his students who was in the final semester of his senior year. The student had filed for graduation and his parents had bought their plane tickets for the big event. However, the student was caught plagiarizing on a paper and received an "F" in the class. He had to sit and watch his friends graduate, while he planned summer school.[41]

Is it easy to cheat and get away with it? Based on statistics and the number of students who actually get caught, I'd say "yes." However, even if you are sly and can get away with it, cheating is still not worth it. When you cheat, you never really learn the information and skills you are supposed to learn. And, although it seems that there is a lot to be gained by getting correct answers unethically, if you cheat, you are cheating yourself. You set the groundwork for failure and rob yourself of the joy of accomplishment and the peace and self-confidence that come from doing your best. In an article entitled "Cheating in the Classroom: Beyond Policing," Dr. Daniel Lee tells the story of one of his acquaintances, who was a classmate of his through the first twelve years of formal education. Although Lee's classmate paid the price for cheating up through high school, cheating in college is no different. You will pay the price.

> When I saw her at a class reunion a few years ago, she boasted about cheating all through elementary school and high school. She did not say much, however, about her career experiences once she graduated high school. The zenith of her career was serving as a short-order cook in a greasy spoon

restaurant. By cheating her way through school, she cheated herself out of an education, which significantly limited her career possibilities when she graduated from high school. In short, the person shortchanged the most by cheating is almost always the cheater.[42]

Preparation is the key. When you are not prepared, there is the temptation to compromise your integrity and to make yourself look better than what you really are. The fear of failure, or the fear of not making the grade, makes it extremely tempting to cheat and take the easy way out. "It's no big deal," you say. "Everyone else does it anyway." Well, let's say you develop heart problems. You experience a heart attack and go in for emergency open-heart surgery. Do you want a surgeon to operate on you who cheated to get through med school? It is a big deal.

College is a chance to learn and prepare for your future, and if you start taking shortcuts, you will only hurt yourself. If you cheat and get by once, what's going to stop you the next time? If you cheat on small things, you are going to cheat on bigger things. And, if you start compromising on even one part of your life, your integrity and self-worth immediately start to deteriorate. Sooner or later your fraud will catch up to you. Don't let a simple GPA steal away your self-worth. Be a real man or woman, and don't cheat!

Lesson 49 |

Honesty Is Still the Best Policy

There are few things better than doing your absolute best and successfully accomplishing your goal. It is a great feeling to know there was an obstacle in your path–whether it was exercising, finishing a paper, or graduating from college–and you conquered it fair and square. Overcoming any obstacle or conquering any goal, at first, may seem overwhelming. It may appear to be too large of a task. However, overcoming any obstacle or conquering any goal is not a matter of completing one big task. Rather, it is simply completing small, individual tasks on a daily basis. Soon, those small, individual tasks add up, and the job is done and the goal is accomplished. A semester is not a big chunk of time or a huge amount of information. Rather, it is roughly seventy-five individual days of going to class, taking notes, studying those notes, completing the reading assignments, and doing the homework. Each classroom assignment is a piece of a big puzzle, and if you cut corners, or compromise your effort, or cheat on even the smallest of tasks, you will rob yourself of the immense gratification that could be yours. However, if you will be honest with yourself and honest in your effort in even the smallest of tasks, you will truly enjoy a tremendous amount of peace and satisfaction that is hard to beat.

As I mentioned in the previous lesson, preparation is the key. If you are prepared, there is no need to cheat or take shortcuts. And, if you diligently follow **The 4 Study Steps**, you should be extremely prepared. It is an awesome feeling walking into the classroom on the day of the test, full of well-earned confidence, knowing that you are about to tee off on whatever the professor puts in front of you. That same feeling can be yours. So, do your own work and hold your head high. No fear. No guilt. No apologies. Be a man or woman of Excellence, and you can truly enjoy your academic victories.

Lesson 50 |

It Ain't Over 'til the Fat Lady Sings!

Finish school!

Lesson 51 |

Reasons Why It Ain't Over 'til the Fat Lady Sings!

In my experience as Assistant Director of Admissions, I've seen many students who weren't sure what they wanted to major in, so they decided to stay home and work until they knew for sure. The majority of those students then got jobs that paid more than what they were making in high school and saw paying for college, not as an investment, but as an unnecessary expense. Even though they knew they could get their college degree and probably earn quite a bit more money than what they were currently making and enjoy benefits they didn't currently have, they wouldn't make the transition. They later married and had families of their own. Years later, when they wanted to go back to school, they found it was one of the toughest things they had ever tried to do.[43]

So, if you're contemplating sitting out a semester or taking a year off because you don't know what direction you want to go or what area of study you want to pursue, please don't! Take at least one class and keep going toward your goal of completing your degree. If you take a semester off now, it will be easier to rationalize taking off another semester next year. You never know what the future holds. Before long, life will happen and you'll wish you would have finished school.

Believe me. It will never be easier to go to college than right out of high school. Just ask the millions of Americans who are trying to go back to finish a degree while working a full-time job and raising a family that desperately needs their time. Do you think that going back to school is fun for them? I guarantee they wish they had finished the first time around.

Lesson 52 |

"I Wish I Had Known This Earlier!"

My first real job out of college was working as an accountant in St. Louis. When I interviewed for this position, I was a little surprised at how the interview went. After all, I had never interviewed for a full-time job, so it was all new to me. What surprised me were the topics of discussion and what the prospective employer seemed to deem as most important in determining whether or not he would hire me. What do employers really want from college grads? I am going to share some information with you that I wish someone in my high school had shared with me before I even set foot in my dorm room my freshman year of college.

We live in a very competitive marketplace, and whatever you can do to set yourself apart from the other interviewees will definitely help your cause. I used to think you had to have a very high GPA to land the good jobs and those with a low GPA had to settle for whatever scraps were left over. However, one of my Accounting professors informed me that that is not entirely true. He said that having a solid GPA will show that you are teachable and that you have enough discipline to get the work done, but it will not be a free ticket for a job. Prospective employers want someone who is competent and who can interact well and communicate well with others. They would rather have a graduate who had decent grades (3.25 or higher) and who was involved in a few organizations than a 4.0 student who sat in his or her room and studied all the time.[44]

Another professor revealed to me that employers and graduate schools are looking for students who have undertaken something above and beyond the normal course load—something extra, such as an internship or a special research project. With so many "A" students graduating from college, those with extra experience get the extra attention.[45]

Book knowledge and classroom knowledge are good, but you will find that actual job experience is going to be very different than the classroom setting. Employers realize they can teach you what you need to know on the job to be successful, so in every interview I went through, the employer spent the majority of the time asking me about myself, the activities and organizations I was involved in, and how I could help his or her company. The interviewer only spent a moment on my grades, and that was it.

So, my advice to you is to do your very best in the classroom *and* get involved in only as many activities and organizations as you have time for, that you really support, and that will help you develop new skills or acquire a deeper knowledge. These criteria are very important in deciding where to spend your extra time. Don't take on responsibilities or join a group just because a bunch of your friends are joining or because it will "look good on your resume." You will spend plenty of your precious time in meetings and events, so make sure you are committed before you sign up.

My Accounting professor also recommended taking on some leadership role such as President, Vice-President, Secretary, Treasurer, Manager, or Assistant Manager in some of these organizations. This will help set you apart and show your future employer that you can effectively take on responsibility and are willing to get out of your comfort zone.[46] More importantly, it will help in the development of your interaction and communication skills, help you meet more people, and even develop long-lasting memories and relationships.

Now, before you go and sign up for President of several organizations, let me tell you a few things I've noticed by being on a college campus for many years. While hundreds of students have come through my office, only a few of them really got my attention. I have been very impressed by those students who seemed to know what they wanted, even before they set foot on campus. And, even if they really didn't know what direction to take in their life, they knew what their values were and they really didn't care what other people thought of them. They had a sense of confidence and maturity about them that was beyond their peers.

Over the next several years, these students got really involved in other people's lives and they built deep relationships with only a handful of people. They were also heavily involved in a few organizations and took on leadership roles in one or two of them, but they didn't go after every organization on campus. They weren't concerned with the social or political status of being a leader and didn't feel the need to be in a leadership position in every organization they were in. In fact, they became involved simply because they wanted to help. They wanted to serve other people. They knew they didn't have to be at the top to be important. If they could help just one person, they were successful.

When I look back on my college years, I know I did not have that mindset and I regret going after the wrong things. I felt I had to be involved in many organizations and take on leadership responsibilities in those organizations just so people would respect me more. However, had I respected myself more initially and not worried so much about what other people thought, I would not have even signed up for half of those organizations and not allowed myself to get spread so thin. That would have freed up quite a bit of time to get more deeply involved with my friends and other people and would have allowed me to serve more when the need arose. And helping others, I have found, is one of the real keys to having a successful college career and a wonderful adventure in the years that follow.

So, in conclusion, let me encourage you to do just that. Just as you should keep your eyes open for odd moments to study throughout the day, you should also be on the lookout for opportunities to be helpful to those who could use a little assistance, especially to those who can't repay the favor. Start looking around. You will find many opportunities to serve in some capacity–sometimes to your closest friends, sometimes to total strangers. I know that by helping someone, whoever it may be and whatever his or her situation, you will receive a much bigger benefit than the benefit you are giving away. It works every time.

I hope you have an awesome college experience, and may God bless you richly in all you do!

Sincerely,

Mark Pruitt

I'd love to hear your comments and success stories:
pruittmark@yahoo.com.

Appendix A

Quiz #1
Answer

❖ ❖ ❖

Wﾞhen classes are over, you need to be studying at your Study Zone. You say, "No thanks. I've got to study. Maybe some other time." And then, when class gets out, you go straight to your Study Zone to complete **Study Steps 2–4**.

Appendix B

Quiz #2
Answer

❖ ❖ ❖

Should you go watch the movie? It all depends. Have you completed **Study Step 2** by studying all the notes from the day, plus all the previous days' notes in every class? Have you then completed **Study Step 3** by doing all your reading? And, what about **Study Step 4**? Have you completed all of your homework assignments or put some time into an upcoming project?

If the answer to any of the above questions is "No," then your answer to the movie is "No." One exception to this rule, however, is if you are in need of a Grande study break.

I am definitely not against watching a movie with your friends, but there is a time for that and now may not be that time. However, if you are disciplined with your time, you may be able to get your studying done before evening, and then you can watch your movie guilt-free.

But if you're not done studying, ask them to wait until later. If they really want you to join them, they may wait. They may not. They may give you a hard time, but stick to your guns. Your discipline may encourage one of your buddies to get to studying, too.

Appendix C

Quiz #3
Answer

❖ ❖ ❖

The first thing you need to do is get out your notebook and go over the notes you took for the day and review the notes from all previous classes (**Study Step 2**). If you have the desire to listen to music or watch TV, use those as a study break. Your first priority should be to study your classroom notes. Even if your body is screaming to take a nap, fight it. Discipline yourself to study your notes first, and then sleep. If you sleep before studying your notes, you will wipe out any Window of Recovery.

Appendix D

Quiz #4
Answer

❖ ❖ ❖

T he first step is to check the time budget you set up this morning. It lists several items that still need to get done:

Study notes – :30

Reading – 1:15

Homework/Project – :15

Laundry – 2:00

Get ready for date – 1:00

Total – 5:00

Remember that, although it is Friday afternoon, to be successful, you still need to go through **The 4 Study Steps** like you normally would, but only until 5:00 or 5:30 pm. Since it is 2:00 pm, and your date begins at 6:00 pm, you have four hours to complete five hours of work.

Because you only have four hours, the next step is to look for areas where you can shave off time. Since studying is your main activity, you don't want to cut it short, and realistically, you know it will probably take you a full hour to get ready for your date. That leaves the laundry. Can you get the laundry done in one hour instead of two? If not, could you work on your laundry for an hour today and do the other hour tomorrow? Or, will you need to re-schedule it all for tomorrow? Fortunately, laundry is one of those activities you can do while working on something else, so nothing has to be cut back. However, if you had an activity that couldn't be done while simultaneously working on something else, then you need to decide which activity is going to get cut and moved to a later opportunity.

So, you get your books and your dirty laundry and off to the laundromat you go. While the clothes are washing, you use this time to study the notes from today's classes and all previous classes. Since you used your odd moments wisely and studied most of your notes throughout the day, you are able to complete **Study Step 2** in about twenty to thirty minutes. You then begin **Study Step 3** by opening your textbook and doing your reading assignment. You read until your laundry is done, and then pack up and head to your Study Zone. You don't spend this time watching TV or playing computer games. Instead, you continue to work on **Study Step 3** and **Study Step 4** until 5:00 pm. At this point, you quit studying for the night. You then get ready for your date and have a great time, knowing that you have done your very best and have gotten a lot accomplished.

Notes |

1. N. Lincoln Hanks, interview by author, Malibu, CA,
    December 31, 2009.

2. John Medina, *Brain Rules*, Pear Press (CD), 2008; C.H. Morgan,
    J.D. Lilley, and N.C. Boreham, "Learning from Lectures: The
    Effect of Varying the Detail in Lecture Handouts on Note-
    taking and Recall," *Applied Cognitive Psychology* 2, no. 2 (April/
    June 1988): 121.

3. Brian Green, "The Conscious and Subconscious Mind:
    Influence, Persuasion & Change for Healing with Hypnosis
    & Hypnotherapy," http://hypnosishealthinfo.com/articles/the-
    conscious-and-subconscious-mind-influence-persuasion-change-
    for-healing-with-hypnosis-hypnotherapy (accessed July 8, 2014).

4. Patricia Flokis, "Affirmations," *Good Health* (October 2013):
    156-158; Zig Ziglar, *See You at the Top*, Nightingale-Conant
    Corporation (audiocassette), 1985; Napoleon Hill, *Think and Grow
    Rich*, Audio Renaissance (audiocassette), 1987.

5. Mark Bohay, Daniel P. Blakely, Andrea K. Tamplin, and
    Gabriel A. Radvansky, "Note taking, Review, Memory, and
    Comprehension," *The American Journal of Psychology* 124,
    no. 1 (Spring 2011): 63-73.

6. Gui Xue, Leilei Mei, Chuansheng Chen, Zhong-Lin Lu, Russell Poldrack, and Qi Dong, "Spaced Learning Enhances Subsequent Recognition Memory by Reducing Neural Repetition Suppression," *Journal of Cognitive Neuroscience* 23, no. 7 (July 2011): 1624-1633.

7. Brian Tracy, *The Psychology of Achievement*, Simon & Schuster, Inc. (CD), 1994.

8. Penn State University, Penn State Learning, "Note Taking," Penn State University, https://pennstatelearning.psu.edu/note-taking (accessed June 14, 2014).

9. Mortimer J. Adler and Charles Van Doren, *How to Read a Book* (New York: Simon and Schuster, 1972), 46-47.

10. Ibid., 46-47.

11. Ibid., 48-51.

12. Ibid., 40-41.

13. Brian Tracy, *The Psychology of Achievement*, Simon & Schuster, Inc. (CD), 1994.

14. Mortimer J. Adler and Charles Van Doren, *How to Read a Book* (New York: Simon and Schuster, 1972), 40-41.

15. P.W. Gillett, "Abraham Lincoln's Financial Troubles & Obstacles to Get to the White House," http://www.bakersfieldlaw.org/id28.html (accessed October 5, 2009).

16. Penn State University, Penn State Learning, "Academic Success," Penn State University, http://dus.psu.edu/academicsuccess/explanation.html (accessed June 14, 2014).

17. John Medina, *Brain Rules*, Pear Press (CD), 2008; C.H. Morgan, J.D. Lilley, and N.C. Boreham, "Learning from Lectures: The Effect of Varying the Detail in Lecture Handouts on Note-taking and Recall," *Applied Cognitive Psychology* 2, no. 2 (1988): 121.

18. Jennifer T. Freeland, Christopher H. Skinner, Bertha Jackson, C. Elizabeth McDaniel, and Stephanie Smith, "Measuring and Increasing Silent Reading Comprehension Rates: Empirically Validating a Repeated Readings Intervention," *Psychology in the Schools* 37, no. 5 (September 2000): 419.

19. R. Davidhizar, V.L. Poole, and N. Giger, "Power Nap Rejuvenates Body, Mind," *Pennsylvania Nurse* 51, (March 1996): 6-7; Harvey B. Simon, "Caught Napping," *Harvard Men's Health Watch* 13, no. 2 (September 2008): 8.

20. Zig Ziglar, *See You at the Top*, Nightingale-Conant Corporation (audiocassette), 1985.

21. Sam Walton, *Made in America* (New York: Doubleday Dell Publishing Group, Inc., 1992), 148.

22. Zig Ziglar, *See You at the Top*, Nightingale-Conant Corporation (audiocassette), 1985.

23. *What about Bob?*, directed by Frank Oz, Touchstone Pictures in association with Touchwood Pacific Partners 1, 1991.

24. *A Christmas Story*, directed by Bob Clark, Christmas Tree Films and Metro-Goldwyn-Mayer, 1983.

25. Catherine A. Hawkins, Michael L. Smith, Raymond C. Hawkins II, and Darlene Grant, "The Relationships Among Hours Employed, Perceived Work Interference, and Grades as Reported by Undergraduate Social Work Students," *Journal of Social Work Education* 41, no. 1 (Winter 2005): 22-24.

26. Dictionary.com, http://dictionary.reference.com/browse/ discourage (accessed September 20, 2009).

27. Ranjita Misra and Michelle McKean, "College Students' Academic Stress and Its Relation to Their Anxiety, Time Management, and Leisure Satisfaction," *American Journal of Health Studies* 16, no. 1 (2000): 41.

28. Brian Tracy, *The Psychology of Achievement*, Simon & Schuster, Inc. (CD), 1994.

29. Jim Rohn, *The Art of Exceptional Living*, Simon & Schuster, Inc. (CD), 1994.

30. Ken Buch, "Brain Break: Understanding the Influence of Brain Functions on Organizational Effectiveness," *T+D* 64, no. 5 (May 2010): 42-47.

31. Brian Tracy, *The Psychology of Achievement*, Simon & Schuster, Inc. (CD), 1994.

32. Brian Tracy, *The Psychology of Achievement*, Simon & Schuster, Inc. (CD), 1994.

33. Karen Vail-Smith, W. Michael Felts, and Craig Becker, "Relationship Between Sleep Quality and Health Risk Behaviors in Undergraduate College Students," *College Student Journal* 43, no. 3 (September 2009), under "Discussion," http://nexus.harding.edu:2054/ehost/detail?vid=104&hid=8&sid=8fcff3d1-3f26-41dd-960d-2e8c3a6bad12%40sessionmgr12&bdata=JmxvZ2luLmFzcCZzaXRlP WVob3N0LWxpdmU%3d#db=aph&AN=43969294 (accessed November 4, 2009); Aparna Nancherla, "You Snooze, You Learn," *T+D* 63, no. 2 (February 2009): 18.

34. Fernando Gomez-Pinilla, "Brain Foods: The Effects of Nutrients on Brain Function," *Nature Reviews Neuroscience* 9, no. 7 (July 2008): 572-575.

35. John Guiliana and Hal Ornstein, "Fit for Success," *Podiatry Management* 30, no. 9 (November/December 2011): 241-242; Zig Ziglar, *See You at the Top*, Nightingale-Conant Corporation (audiocassette), 1985.

36. Charles H. Hillman, Kirk I. Erickson, and Arthur F. Kramer, "Be Smart, Exercise Your Heart: Exercise Effects on Brain and Cognition," *Nature Reviews Neuroscience* 9, no. 1 (January 2008): 58-63; Martin T. Woodlee and Timothy Schallert, "The Impact of Motor Activity and Inactivity on the Brain: Implications for the Prevention and Treatment of Nervous-system Disorders," *Current Directions in Psychological Science* 15, no. 4 (August 2006): 204.

37. Jonathan Guez and Moshe Naveh-Benjamin, "Divided Attention at Encoding and Retrieval for Once- and Thrice-presented Items: A Micro-level Analysis of Attentional Costs," *European Journal of Cognitive Psychology* 18, no. 6 (November 2006): 884.

38. Mike Plummer, interview by author, Searcy, AR, June 3, 2010.

39. Daniel E. Lee, "Cheating in the Classroom: Beyond Policing," *Clearing House* 82, no. 4 (March/April 2009): 171.

40. Chris Bates, "A Student's View: Why Cheating Matters," *Chronicle of Higher Education* 55, no. 24 (February 20, 2009), under "Commentary," http://nexus.harding.edu:2054/ehost/detail?vid=101&hid=8&sid=8fcff3d1-3f26-41dd-960d-2e8c3a6bad12%40sessionmgr12&bdata=JmxvZ2luLmFzcCZzaXRlPWVob3N0LWxpdmU%3d#db=aph&AN=36815883 (accessed January 28, 2010).

41. B. Cole Bennett, interview by author, Abilene, TX, February 2, 2010.

42. Daniel E. Lee, "Cheating in the Classroom: Beyond Policing," *Clearing House* 82, no. 4 (March/April 2009): 172.

43. Jennifer Kohier Giancola, Matthew J. Grawitch, and Dana Borchert, "Dealing with the Stress of College: A Model for Adult Students," *Adult Education Quarterly* 59, no. 3 (May 2009): 257-258.

44. Mike Emerson, interview by author, Searcy, AR, March 17, 1992.

45. Mike Plummer, interview by author, Searcy, AR, June 3, 2010.

46. Mike Emerson, interview by author, Searcy, AR, March 17, 1992.

Bibliography |

Adler, Mortimer J., and Charles Van Doren. *How to Read a Book.* New York: Simon and Schuster, 1972.

Bates, Chris. "A Student's View: Why Cheating Matters." *Chronicle of Higher Education* 55, no. 24 (February 20, 2009). http://nexus. harding.edu:2054/ehost/detail?vid=101&hid=8&sid=8fcff3d1-3f26- 41dd-960d-2e8c3a6bad12%40sessionmgr12&bdata=JmxvZ2luLm FzcCZzaXRlPWVob3N0LWxpdmU%3d#db=aph&AN=36815883 (accessed January 28, 2010).

Bohay, Mark, Daniel P. Blakely, Andrea K. Tamplin, and Gabriel A. Radvansky. "Note taking, Review, Memory, and Comprehension." *The American Journal of Psychology* 124, no. 1 (Spring 2011): 63-73.

Buch, Ken. "Brain Break: Understanding the Influence of Brain Functions on Organizational Effectiveness." *T+D* 64, no. 5 (May 2010): 42-47.

Davidhizar, R., V.L. Poole, and N. Giger. "Power Nap Rejuvenates Body, Mind." *Pennsylvania Nurse* 51 (March 1996): 6-7.

Dictionary.com. http://dictionary.reference.com/browse/discourage (accessed September 20, 2009).

Flokis, Patricia. "Affirmations." *Good Health* (October 2013): 156-158.

Freeland, Jennifer T., Christopher H. Skinner, Bertha Jackson, C. Elizabeth McDaniel, and Stephanie Smith. "Measuring and Increasing Silent Reading Comprehension Rates: Empirically Validating a Repeated Readings Intervention." *Psychology in the Schools* 37, no. 5 (September 2000): 415-429.

Giancola, Jennifer Kohier, Matthew J. Grawitch, and Dana Borchert. "Dealing with the Stress of College: A Model for Adult Students." *Adult Education Quarterly* 59, no. 3 (May 2009): 246-263.

Gillett, P.W. "Abraham Lincoln's financial troubles & obstacles to get to the White House." http://www.bakersfieldlaw.org/id28.html (accessed October 5, 2009).

Gomez-Pinilla, Fernando. "Brain Foods: The Effects of Nutrients on Brain Function." *Nature Reviews Neuroscience* 9, no. 7 (July 2008): 568-578.

Green, Brian. "The Conscious and Subconscious Mind: Influence, Persuasion & Change for Healing with Hypnosis & Hypnotherapy." http://hypnosishealthinfo.com/articles/the-conscious-and-subconscious-mind-influence-persuasion-change-for-healing-with-hypnosis-hypnotherapy (accessed July 8, 2014).

Guez, Jonathan, and Moshe Naveh-Benjamin. "Divided Attention at Encoding and Retrieval for Once- and Thrice-presented Items: A Micro-level Analysis of Attentional Costs." *European Journal of Cognitive Psychology* 18, no. 6 (November 2006): 874-898.

Guiliana, John, and Hal Ornstein. "Fit for Success." *Podiatry Management* 30, no. 9 (November/December 2011): 241-242.

Hawkins, Catherine A., Michael L. Smith, Raymond C. Hawkins II, and Darlene Grant. "The Relationships Among Hours Employed, Perceived Work Interference, and Grades as Reported by Undergraduate Social Work Students." *Journal of Social Work Education* 41, no. 1 (Winter 2005): 13-27.

Hill, Napoleon. *Think and Grow Rich.* Excerpts read by the author. Los Angeles: Audio Renaissance. Audiocassette. 1987.

Hillman, Charles H., Kirk I. Erickson, and Arthur F. Kramer. "Be Smart, Exercise Your Heart: Exercise Effects on Brain and Cognition." *Nature Reviews Neuroscience* 9, no. 1 (January 2008): 58-65.

Lee, Daniel E. "Cheating in the Classroom: Beyond Policing." *Clearing House* 82, no. 4 (March/April 2009): 171-176.

Medina, John. *Brain Rules.* Seattle: Pear Press. CD. 2008.

Misra, Ranjita, and Michelle McKean. "College Students' Academic Stress and Its Relation to Their Anxiety, Time Management, and Leisure Satisfaction." *American Journal of Health Studies* 16, no. 1 (2000): 41-51.

Morgan, C.H., J.D. Lilley, and N.C. Boreham. "Learning from Lectures: The Effect of Varying the Detail in Lecture Handouts on Note-taking and Recall." *Applied Cognitive Psychology* 2, no. 2 (April/June 1988): 115-122.

Nancherla, Aparna. "You Snooze, You Learn." *T+D* 63, no. 2 (February 2009): 18.

Penn State University, Penn State Learning. "Academic Success." Penn State University. http://dus.psu.edu/academicsuccess/explanation.html (accessed June 14, 2014).

Penn State University, Penn State Learning. "Note Taking." Penn State University. https://pennstatelearning.psu.edu/note-taking (accessed June 14, 2014).

Rohn, Jim. *The Art of Exceptional Living.* New York: Simon & Schuster, Inc. CD. 1994.

Simon, Harvey B. "Caught Napping." *Harvard Men's Health Watch* 13, no. 2 (September 2008): 8.

Tracy, Brian. *The Psychology of Achievement.* New York: Simon & Schuster, Inc. CD. 1994.

Vail-Smith, Karen, W. Michael Felts, and Craig Becker. "Relationship Between Sleep Quality and Health Risk Behaviors in Undergraduate College Students." *College Student Journal* 43, no. 3 (September 2009). http://nexus.harding.edu:2054/ehost/detail?vid=104&hid=8&sid=8fcff3d1-3f26-41dd-960d-2e8c3a6bad12%40sessionmgr12&bdata=JmxvZ2luLmFzcCZzaXRlPWVob3N0LWxxpdmU%3d#db=aph&AN=43969294 (accessed November 4, 2009).

Walton, Sam M. *Made in America.* New York: Doubleday Dell Publishing Group, Inc., 1992.

Woodlee, Martin T., and Timothy Schallert. "The Impact of Motor Activity and Inactivity on the Brain: Implications for the Prevention and Treatment of Nervous-system Disorders." *Current Directions in Psychological Science* 15, no. 4 (August 2006): 203-206.

Xue, Gui, Leilei Mei, Chuansheng Chen, Zhong-Lin Lu, Russell Poldrack, and Qi Dong. "Spaced Learning Enhances Subsequent Recognition Memory by Reducing Neural Repetition Suppression." *Journal of Cognitive Neuroscience* 23, no. 7 (July 2011): 1624-1633.

Ziglar, Zig. *See You at the Top.* Chicago: Nightingale-Conant Corporation. Audiocassette. 1985.